THE UNLEARNED LESSONS
OF THE TWENTIETH CENTURY

CROSSCURRENTS

ISI Books' Crosscurrents series makes available in English, usually for the first time, new translations of both classic and contemporary works by authors working within, or with crucial importance for, the conservative, religious, and humanist intellectual traditions.

Titles in series

Icarus Fallen, by Chantal Delsol, trans. by Robin Dick

Critics of the Enlightenment, ed. and trans. by Christopher O. Blum

Equality by Default, by Philippe Bénéton, trans. by Ralph C. Hancock

Editorial advisory board

THE UNLEARNED LESSONS

OF THE

TWENTIETH CENTURY

AN ESSAY ON LATE MODERNITY

Chantal Delsol

TRANSLATED BY Robin Dick

ISI Books
WILMINGTON, DELAWARE
2006

Delsol, Chantal, 1947–

The unlearned lessons of the twentieth century : an essay on late modernity / Chantal Delsol ; translated by Robin Dick. — 1st ed. — Wilmington, Del. : ISI Books, 2006.

p. ; cm.

ISBN-13: 978-1-932236-46-0
ISBN-13: 978-1-932236-47-7 (pbk.)
ISBN-10: 1-932236-46-5
ISBN-10: 1-932236-47-3 (pbk.)
Includes bibliographical references and index.

1. Philosophy and civilization. 2. Philosophy, Modern—21st century. 3. Humanism. 4. Postmodernism. I. Dick, Robin. II. Title.

B59 .D45 2006
306.01—dc22   0607

Library of Congress Control Number: 2006925554

Book design by Kathryn Smith

Published in the United States by:

ISI Books
Intercollegiate Studies Institute
Post Office Box 4431
Wilmington, DE 19807-0431
www.isibooks.org

CONTENTS

CHAPTER 1
INTRODUCTION

Imagine an heir who has just been informed that his inheritance consists of a trunk full of serpents.

Such is our situation at the turn of the century. The twentieth century, born in the worship of the future, is now ending with shame for the past and contempt for the future. Having been too often betrayed by our expectations, we look upon any idea of promise as a virtual betrayal. If hope can be compared to a well in a garden, it is as if we now felt that the well had been poisoned.

The rejection of hope manifests itself in two psychological reactions: The first consists in a revolt against those realities which, with the failure of totalitarian utopias, proved inescapable. Faced with the fact that the twentieth century was unable to produce an ideal society, we cry, "If human society is to remain imperfect until the end of time, then to the devil with hope: let us have utopia or nothing!" The second reaction consists in a wish to remain stock-still in the situation of freedom and well-being in which we find ourselves, thereby avoiding the temptation to embrace expectations that will once again turn out to be fruitless and dangerous.

And so hope today consists in doing without hope, of simply living without it. But is this really possible? Is it conceivable that man should be transformed to the point of no longer having a need for meaning? Could life's happiness henceforth be found in the absence of meaning? These questions have become common, and the supposed answer to them is yes. This is why it is not surprising that we sift through time and search beyond borders to see if societies, in previous times or elsewhere, might have lived or might still live without this strange thing called hope. This would account for the current fascination with Stoicism and Asian thought. One might even say that these two different philosophical expressions of self-sufficiency have been instrumentalized, reinterpreted with the express purpose of demonstrating that a society without hope remains viable. Hopelessness is renamed "non-hopefulness" in order to make the term somehow more optimistic or volitional.

To seek no more than what is "acceptable" or "in conformity with nature" is what links the Stoic to the Chinese philosopher (or at least what the West knows of Chinese philosophers). This is precisely what our moment in late modernity is looking for. The loss of collective undertakings must now be seen not as a harmful defection, but as the dawn of a new era ushered in by a new humanity. And so we are led to believe (and this idea is to be found as much in literature and sectarian theories as it is in philosophy) that the Chinese sage was able to do without a self, being, truth, meaning, logic, or any teleology whatsoever. In the presence of this belief, the postmodern self feels reassured and vindicated, living as he does in the banishment of truths, universals, and purpose. His nothingness finds, or at least believes it has found, an echo in the nothingness of age-old Chinese philosophy. In this sense, he believes that he represents a new form of being—not a lack of being. From now on he will be able to do without meaning and a future; he will live in the immobility of the present.

But beyond postmodern theory, what can history and geography teach us about the possibility that a society might live without hope?

After all, most ancient human societies lived without any particular hope of improving their world, and even less of changing existence itself. They simply *lived*, and were content to continue in the ways and thoughts of their ancestors. They did not foresee for themselves a future beyond the next two or three generations. Even today, most non-Western societies would still live this way if the European idea of progress had not led them to expect, as a society, a better life, or "development."

After an accumulation of disappointed expectations, might we be in the process of turning back toward ancient times, times in which men were content to live out their daily lives without the expectation of a better future? If this were true, it would be a sort of relief, for it would mean that our common existence could find safe haven in the past without necessarily having to hope for a better life—which, for the time being, escapes definition.

And yet it appears that we cannot reassure ourselves with this escape mechanism. For ancient pre-European and non-European societies recognized a collective meaning, even if this meaning was not written into concrete historical temporality. They of course did not await the end of the world or the return of Christ, as did the Christians of the first few centuries, or a radiant future, as did the masses of the twentieth century. Still, their daily labor and the monotonous renewal of generations found meaning for itself in myth, religion, and wisdom. Without projecting hope onto a collective future, they no less hoped that each community would achieve itself *in the order of things*, in keeping with the community's view of the world and man's place in it. The religions, wisdom, and moral codes of ancient societies may seem to have been fixed in a frozen immortality, at least with respect to modern ways of thinking, but every event and every act sought its meaning within a cultural world in which time had its place.

Of course, the end of messianic and ideological expectations brings us back down to a day-to-day existence in which the only thing left is to live well; such a life includes material comforts and protections of all sorts. But if we were henceforth to wish to live without plans for the future, we would have to reappropriate the spiritual dimension through which life takes on meaning and goes beyond itself, even within daily existence. By contrast, the society of well-being alone, without hope or expectations, locks us into the material world and makes of us the sad heroes of emptiness.

Our present despair reveals the impossibility of living simultaneously in a world inherited from previous centuries and in the dream world of utopias: the former has been renounced and the latter has been definitively proved unachievable. Thus dissolves the common world of a society that now comes together only to celebrate its self-contempt, as seen in its revolt against the past, religious or totalitarian, and its revolt against reality restored, which, by its invasive presence, reveals the horrible excesses of utopias. A whole body of literature has arisen to vomit up the crimes of previous eras. It is as if the only thing that suits us anymore is what stands for the opposite of yesteryear and yesterday.

A new culture, a new way of living and thinking is slowly springing up in the fertile ground of these successive rejections:

- The linear and progressive march of time is giving way to fantasies of cyclical time. The steps of time, promises of progress and of limitless development, are being challenged and gradually replaced by the wheel of time, the eternal return of the same.
- Visions of what society might be are fading along with the idea of the future, which has become mere futurity. The individual clings to the ephemeral moment because he either cannot or does not want to define a purpose to which he might devote his fervor.
- Work as a way of shaping the world, as in the Promethean myth, is giving way to an apologetics of leisure or even of idleness, which is not contemplation but a willed and resigned quietude.

- The common vision of family based on father- and mother-hood is giving way to a preapproved pattern of tribal relationships, devoid of hierarchy and durable, exclusive bonds.
- The idea that man has primacy over nature is being replaced by the equal valuation of all living things—including even inanimate reality, such as space and place.

This culture may be referred to as "late modernity," just as there was a "late antiquity." Even if it is impossible really to compare the present and the distant past, the expression comes to mind for more than one reason. Characterizing the present is always difficult. The expression *postmodernity* carries an ideological connotation: a rejection of the old world, and a consideration of the transformations underway as already completed and ratified. The idea of late modernity, by contrast, merely suggests the end of a cycle, without prejudging any possible turns of events or rebirths. It is late—this means that we are old, which indeed we are. But we cannot infer from this the idea of decadence, at least if we genuinely wish to distance ourselves from the phobia of decline that was so pervasive in the nineteenth and early twentieth centuries: nostalgia has never nourished any culture, except through fits of aggression and revenge, as one might artificially drug a beaten animal. In this respect, we gain from the concept of late antiquity, which has recently replaced that of the Roman Empire in decline,[1] the precious understanding of a mature or old era, without any pejorative connotation attached to the word "old." The concept of lateness does not express—at least not exclusively—a deterioration, an abandonment, or a sort of lassitude: it rather tells of the beginning of the replacement of one culture with another. The late hour of a historical time period is not like the weariness of old age: lateness in time is subverted time. Because cultures, in contrast to men, never really die, in an advanced age a birth takes place in the wake of the overthrow of the old. This birth presupposes the advent of a new age.

Late antiquity—that is, the Roman era from the third to the sixth centuries—shows all the signs of institutional decline, in the sense Plato meant when he stated that every institution ends up dying through the excess of its own principle. In this case it was death through excessive centralization, crushing taxation, and the triumph of a rationality that gave rise to injustice through its sheer inflexibility. It showed all the signs of aging in its affirmation of an art without meaning, a literature that was simultaneously pretentious and trivial, and a dwindling population. But above all, late antiquity heralded, and forcefully so, the advent of that Christian culture which would subsequently give birth to both Byzantine and Occidental civilization. In late antiquity, dawning Christianity subverted the spirit that had prevailed during the post-Republican and early imperial Roman period: the spirit of Stoicism and a diffuse pantheism, the search for happiness in the present moment. The new belief in a sole and transcendent God was bound up with the idea of salvation, which ceased to mean solely the restoration of physical health; it evoked eternal life, with a new vision of historical time, henceforth connected with theology, and the emergence of an affirmed stature for mankind.

In this regard, late modernity does call to mind late antiquity—as an aging world—even as it inverts the content. What emerged during the late Roman Empire—which is to say, what we inherit from Christianity—is today being subverted and replaced by a culture more or less comparable to what was subverted at that time: the Stoicism that had been born earlier amid the ruins of the democratic and republican city and the ideal citizen.

Thus, what was born in late antiquity is precisely what is dying in late modernity: the same European humanism whose end has been proclaimed. But is this to count the chickens before they've hatched, perhaps? This is what I dare hope.

Why reject the new spirit that is now rising from the ashes of the old? Why should we not make new cultural choices, even radically new ones? The answer is because in doing so we would have to give up what we wish to safeguard most of all. Indeed, within the present cultural evolution, which at times seems ineluctable, lies the snag of one immense detail. The society of late modernity, barren and revolted as it may be, is still animated by one common certitude, a conviction that was there at its birth, extends throughout its history, and is perhaps the only thing that remains anchored in its mental *habitus:* the dignity of the individual man. Late modernity cherishes this belief in spite of, even because of the fact that the twentieth century routinely encouraged the suppression of the individual as the "price to pay" for the realization of the future—the terrible notion of "human cost." The revolt against the perversions of European culture is fought in the name of the foundations of that very culture.

The idea of the dignity of the individual rests upon an image of man as a responsible subject and person. The dignity of the individual, that keystone of European culture since its origins (embryonic in ancient Greece, conceptualized by Christianity), rests upon an anthropology which makes of the human being a *person,* an entity possessing a sacred and inalienable value. European culture is the story of the epiphany of the individual who, with the rise of modernity, manifested the concomitant qualities of an autonomous subject, endowed with his own purpose and capable of independence of mind. However, the new ways of thinking and being that are appearing in our societies reject this very anthropology: the self dissipates into a vague pantheism, the subject is subjected to new constraints. In this sense, late modernity, in spite of its claims, has not attempted to replace the totalitarian regimes it has only just rejected: on the contrary, it has become an extension of them by pursuing the effort to efface the subject. Formerly, this had been a prerogative of totalitarian worlds.

Stated otherwise, we wish to escape our demons in order to restore the same human rights of which the past century made a mockery. Yet, in this effort to escape we are in the process of obliterating the very subject who legitimizes those rights. The aim of the present work is to expose this contradiction and its reasons for being: late modernity has rejected the terrorist aspects of totalitarianism, but it has not abandoned the ideological underpinnings of totalitarianism itself.

The key to Europe's future lies in resolving this contradiction. We cling to the certitude of the dignity of the person as a shipwreck victim clings to the overturned ship, because all other certitudes have disappeared or are slowly fading from view. But can the principle of personal dignity be maintained and secured without the cultural world that justifies and sustains it? This principle, the fulcrum of human rights thinking, is not an isolated and insular belief, a concept that can simply stay afloat on its own and find sustenance in nothingness. It finds its legitimacy within an architecture of meaning. The present contradiction, therefore, lies in the subversion of the very culture that sustains our last belief. We will obviously have to find a way out of this dilemma somehow, for if it is indeed possible to think in contradictory terms, it is impossible to live in contradiction without betraying oneself.

The dignity of man as a unique being without substitute is a postulate of faith, not of science. All of history demonstrates its fragility. The collapse of even a section of the immense architecture at the heart of which is the notion of human dignity suffices to weaken its defenses. Personal dignity requires the existence of the person; it requires a subject endowed with conscience and responsibility, one who answers as a witness to his acts; it supposes the moral unity of the human species and the specificity of the human vis-à-vis the animal. The idea of human dignity depends upon an inherited cultural world. Indeed, it was by destroying this heritage that Nazism and communism pulverized it.

Today, we still have not opened our eyes. Instead of shoring up the walls, signposts, and foundations of the principle of personal dignity, we brandish an incantatory and maladapted discourse of human rights. This discourse itself has become an –ism, inhabiting the very ideologies it seeks to combat, and whose work it in reality continues to advance: the destruction of the heritage in which the precarious principle of human dignity resides. A contradictory position to be sure, behind which the breaches of future dehumanizations are already widening: the notion of a *human nonperson* or "human unperson," for example, defended with all the academic seriousness of seductive theories. To ward off totalitarianism, it is not enough to dismiss it; totalitarianism must be replaced. The question of hope then ceases to be an academic debate. If we still have the value of personal dignity to defend, it becomes a question of responsibility: what must we become in order to safeguard that principle? Who is the person-subject, possessor of dignity, and what kind of common world can guarantee his existence?

CHAPTER 2
THE INSULARITY OF THE HUMAN SPECIES

Totalitarianism, of whatever persuasion, emerges when we get caught up in the belief that "everything is possible." It might be worth recalling just how difficult it was to have this idea accepted, or, for instance, to remember how reluctantly the thought of Hannah Arendt was received in France. To deny that "everything is possible," to make the postulate of unlimited possibility the cornerstone of the errors of the century, was, it was said, to equate terror and utopia, or to liken the perversities of man's annihilation to ideals about reshaping human nature. To do this was unthinkable as long as ideological dreams were still so pervasive.

Several decades of perseverant reflection, however, finally made it possible to state openly that the idea that "everything is possible" represents the birth of the twentieth century. This little phrase, which was to reveal itself to be so terrible, essentially means two things. "Everything is possible" is a way of determining who is human: one can then arbitrarily set a boundary here or there between humans and "subhumans" and declare a particular category to be nonhuman, which is what Nazism did. "Everything is possible" is also a way of determining what it is to be human: one can then arbitrarily decree that humans can or should live without authority, without personal secrets, without family, or without gods, which is what communism did. In fact, communism ended up adding the first consequence of "everything is possible" to the second and denied the humanity of those who made no effort to become other than they were.

Nevertheless, as we shall see, the capital importance of "everything is possible" as the foundation of what we hope to avoid at any cost is not recognized as it ought to be. Here and there, some are earnestly trying to revive "everything is possible" in new ways, thus leaving the door ajar to future tyrannies or, in the process, ruining the very world they wish to restore. The same societies that seek to prevent future crimes against humanity harbor new antihumanist currents of thought, the redeployment of which is graciously welcomed. An amused indulgence greets the reemergence of declared enemies of humankind (like the Movement for Voluntary Human Extinction) as well as advocates of new distinctions between grades of humanity, between human persons and "nonpersons." Today, as a century ago, on the question of who is human, it seems that everything is possible.

The irreducible dignity of the human being, our foundational certitude, implies a universal applicability to the species. It presupposes a vast common and primordial world, that of the species of man. Here "men" are considered as a single group in which all individuals, no matter who they are, have the same substantial value. And this group is set apart from other groups—that is, from animal species and the nonliving world.

Because *dignity* is a distinction, the philosophy of human rights rests upon anthropocentrism: no man can have dignity if Man himself is not king of nature. The term "human dignity" means that man may not be treated as a thing: this indicates the essential and radical separation between the human world and the rest of nature and, at the same time, the essential bond between all men.

The biblical account, which lies at the roots of European culture, proposes the appearance of a common ancestor of humanity—Adam.

Whatever the fortunes or misfortunes of monogenesis in the history of science, human unity continues to confirm itself as a structuring tradition. Saint Paul affirmed that all humans, as humans, are alike beyond the criteria of sex, social standing, or ethnic origins. The philosophy of rights later took root in this idea, which from then on was founded upon reason. But whether the postulate of human unity is founded in religion or reason, it still represents the primary idea upon which a world of relationships can be based. In its absence, separation and hatred inevitably arise.

The temptation to dehumanize and the historical attempts to do so stem above all from a rejection of this unity, from a questioning of it, or from troubling debates over the boundaries that define the human species. By indulging in indecision over human status—do Indians have a soul?—the Christians of Europe decimated the populations of America. Las Casas, pleading on the Indians' behalf, did not argue for human dignity (something that was well established in the Christian world). Instead, he began with the premise that Indians are indeed human, hence equal in dignity. (This also constituted the major theme in the controversy of Valladolid.)[1] Dehumanization begins with the denial of human status, with the expulsion of certain humans beyond the frontiers of the species. One cannot brand others as "undeserving" of human dignity without first branding them as "subhuman"—that is, without first dismissing them as radically other.

In the second half of the nineteenth century, the discoveries of biology radically transformed previous certitudes concerning the insularity and specificity of the human species. The biblical account had dug a chasm between man and animal. The theories of evolution brought apes and man so close together as to make the borderline unclear. So unclear, in fact, that the slightest alteration might make it disappear altogether. As Darwin wrote:

> [A]s respects the question of absolute size, it is established that
> the difference between the largest and the smallest healthy hu-

man brain is greater than the difference between the smallest healthy human brain and the largest chimpanzee's or orang's brain.[2]

One can imagine what such a claim might have meant at a time when intelligence was believed to be proportional to brain size. From that point onward, with the religious certitude of mankind's ontological link to God erased, the specificity of humanness disintegrated, and with it, human grandeur and the imperative of respect due every man by virtue of his belonging to the species. The imperative of respect now only held for those who were admitted—by arbitrary criteria?—to membership in the human race. The boundary of respect, having become subjective and therefore fickle, thus came to depend on historical, ideological, or scientific criteria. It no longer necessarily separated man from beast; it could be drawn between different groups of humans, some of which could then be treated as subhumans or as animals.

Eugenics and racism were made possible initially by the blurring of this boundary; they did not so much deny human dignity as they differentiated between humans and others, within a species whose boundaries had become indistinct. As the twentieth century unfolded, the incurably ill, the mentally handicapped, and the asocial were defined as subspecies. Programs of forced sterilization were set up in some American states. Such measures were applauded by many scientists in European countries. In Germany in 1904, a Society for Racial Hygiene was created; as a prelude to the Final Solution, the "asocial," "bastards," the blacks of the Rhineland, and homosexuals underwent forced sterilization while handicapped or retarded children and the mentally ill were gassed.[3] Until the 1970s, "inferior persons," to use the expression of Nils von Hofsten—that is, the physically or socially handicapped—were forcibly sterilized in Sweden.

Could it be that scientific progress inevitably undermines the idea of human uniqueness, allowing all imaginable—or rather, unimaginable—abuses to emerge? No, because the uniqueness of the human species has its roots in nonbiological presuppositions. The divide between human and animal is founded on the creation myth, an ontological account more than an anthropological portrait: man is the animal-friend-of-God, created by God in his image. The prodigious discoveries of nineteenth-century biology could never have provided one of the bases of totalitarianism if the original ontological certitudes had remained intact. Scientific progress was able to sweep away the certainty that the human species is unique because science found itself in charge of establishing certain criteria and definitions after religious messages had lost their legitimacy. Scientism, not science, disunites humanity, and scientism operates through the despotism of a rationality placed above all else.

Many primitive peoples call themselves "the People," which usage expresses the idea of a difference in nature between themselves and others. In other words, the unity and insularity of the human species is a product of culture, a civilized, sophisticated idea, and therefore fragile. The twentieth century is the story of the dismantling of the idea of humanity, a process that gave rise to a disintegration of the essential common world that took so many centuries to build. This disintegration served as the prerequisite and foundation for the possibility of totalitarianism.

Human unity rests upon the certitude of a *divide* between man and animal. The replacement of this divide with *limites*—gray and neutral areas where distinctions are no longer on solid ground—ultimately allows subjectivity to distinguish what is human from what is not. The monstrous consequences of this blurring of lines compels us to sacralize the boundary, to declare its inviolability: With respect to the question "Who is human?" everything is not possible.

And yet late modernity is diligently working to restore *limites*. The temptation to dismantle the idea of humanity is reemerging once again in a climate of indifference.

The scientific work of the past few decades has blurred the distinction between early man and the highly evolved ape to the point of illegibility. What the ape is capable of learning challenges our preconceived notions of the specialness and superiority of our species: he stands upright, recognizes himself in a mirror, learns sign language, uses tools, mourns his dead, and is affected by the unhappiness of his peers. These discoveries would interest science alone if science, as was the case before the nineteenth century, did not believe itself to be the only basis for understanding man's place in the universe. Western opinion, dreading that religious and mythical criteria of human distinction might reemerge, is lapsing into a fascination with the gray zones. It has become fashionable to ardently ridicule any claim about human uniqueness, because such claims have a religious ring to them. However, today's scientism, compared with that of the nineteenth century, has become both hypocritical and worthy of disavowal. In the nineteenth century scientism rested upon the naïve yet understandable belief—since it had not yet clashed with actual experience—that once the religious mentality had been swept aside, science would be able to explain everything and to alone bring happiness to humanity. The twentieth century sufficed to show that this was hardly the case. Thus, the scientism of today is founded on the mere hatred of religion and makes use of its own resentment against good faith. In the nineteenth century no one yet knew to what human catastrophes the "moral collapse that affected the heart of Europe in its entirety"[4] could lead: today we cannot lay claim to such innocence. Today's scientism, when it claims a monopoly on truth and is used to blur the boundaries of the human species, has become virtually criminal.

And so we hear once again claims whose tenor will quickly become troubling if science is left alone to determine our understanding of what man is. The scientific observations of today sound familiarly like Darwinian comparisons: "a chimpanzee can learn up to 800 or 900 words, while certain Creoles understand only 600,"[5] or "some animals can demonstrate a solidarity among themselves which makes them ethically superior to certain *savages*."[6] If we admit only biological factors as acceptable criteria, then when human beings are described biologically there is nothing more to add and distinctions are erased. We owe compassion to animals because they are living beings capable of suffering. We should owe nothing more than this compassion to weak, sick, or suffering human beings whose lives are a burden for themselves and for society. Humanitarian reasons are put forward to justify euthanasia. It is out of compassion that we must kill: a return to an idea that appeared at the end of the nineteenth century, that of a "life that is no longer worth living."

If, as certain ecological currents of thought would have it, the whole of nature can lay claim to the same dignity as man, dignity itself simply vanishes. This dilution is nothing less than a dissolution: if everything has dignity, nothing does, for dignity reflects a distinction. Once this distinction has been rejected, a hierarchy of respect can be established at the whim of reigning ideologies and as dictated by the fears that shape public opinion: some will be deemed less worthy than others.

The Kantian imperatives, which are supposed to provide us with an ethic of respect freed from religious foundations, will not be sufficient to counter the temptation to establish new hierarchies between those who are worthy of respect and those who are not. The Kantian imperative convincingly justifies the respect owed to a human being. According to it, man is a being endowed with moral autonomy; the difference in comparison with the religious requirement of respect is not the requirement itself, but the introduction of criteria by which to designate the group that is owed respect, namely mankind. The mythic-religious tale of the Bible allowed for dignity to be conferred upon every human being, no matter who he was. This effectively warded off, or at least rendered immoral, any attempt to establish distinctions between different groups: man is worthy of dignity no matter what, simply because he is a man, simply because in the story of creation, God chose him. With the Kantian secularization of foundations, the divine choice is replaced by a human quality that makes him superior to the animal, namely, his moral autonomy. It then becomes tempting to say: it is not man who has dignity, but man insofar as he is autonomous.[7]

One characteristic cannot be sufficient to distinguish mankind. When the moderns, under Kant's umbrella, proposed autonomy as the determining quality of what is human, they were wrong to believe that human dignity was thereby safeguarded. For then humans without autonomy—newborns, the dying, the handicapped—could lose their status as human beings. It is possible that only an ontology can save from indignity the groups that every era labels differently as subgroups—the lame of conscience in one era; the rejected peoples of another era. Unless the being of mankind is given serious thought, appearances or phenomena reign, with nothing to check temptations to discriminate. By describing man as an entity that cannot be reduced to his characteristics and limits, European culture wished to save him from historical and circumstantial considerations that might lessen his worth. With this understanding, man has dignity even when he has lost everything: social attributes, intellectual capabilities, even his ability to love. The aged Oedipus, blind, stripped of his royalty and honor, said long ago through the mouth of Sophocles, "It's when there is nothing left of me that I really become a man."[8] Although lacking all means, he remains the being who thirsts for everything, clothed in dignity as if in full glory, just as we see the disinherited person who lived in one of the countless camps of the twentieth century. The very fact that we see him in this way, in spite of all the efforts to rob him of his human attributes, is sufficient indication of the ontological character of dignity.

However, the temptation to draw distinctions on the basis of abilities or definitions is making a comeback today with the new eugenics. Some currents of thought assert the subhumanity or nonhumanity of certain groups because of their lack or loss of abilities. Once this step has been taken, when one reserves the label "person" for the human being who is able to lay claim to full dignity, certain humans become nonpersons or unpersons. "This use of 'person' is itself, unfortunately, liable to mislead, since 'person' is often used as if it meant the same as 'human being.' Yet the terms are not equivalent; there could be a person who is not a member of our species. There could also be members of our species who are not 'persons,'" writes Peter Singer,[9] who reserves use of the word "person" for human beings who are rational and self-aware. Or again, "[N]ot all humans are persons. Not all humans are self-conscious, rational, and able to conceive of the possibility of blaming and praising. Fetuses, infants, the profoundly mentally retarded, and the hopelessly comatose provide examples of human nonpersons."[10] A being without moral autonomy, like a newborn baby, would have no more value than the measure of our attachment to it: those around it would decide what respect to confer upon it, the only obligation being the benevolence owed to a being capable of suffering, whether animal or human.[11]

It is easy to imagine the possible consequences, the abuses that henceforth would be legitimated, were this kind of idea to take root. Between early-twentieth-century eugenics and the genetic engineering of today there is a well-established resemblance that goes beyond their ultimate purposes. "The approach [today] is comparable to the approach taken in the first half of the century, which used such justifications as public health (individual health, today), the degeneracy of the human race (genetic illness, today), and eugenic sterilization (today's genetic therapy, actually screening),"[12] writes André Bichot.

This amounts to selecting those humans worthy of life, who are to be called persons. Who will do this selecting? According to what criteria? The dawning century has much to fear.

Man is not a *product* defined by various characteristics, or a being about which one can say everything there is to be said. Neither individually nor historically is he fully explained by his exegetes. His qualities do not sum him up entirely. If one examines him under a microscope, bit by bit, or peels off layer after layer to try to understand the secret of his being, one will discover nothing more than a piece of meat. Since we categorically refuse to allow him to be treated like a piece of meat, we cannot reduce his specificities to those of science. Beyond biology or paleontology, man is the story of an insurrection against the condition of animal, and a transcendence with respect to nature. And because he conceives of the universe, which does not conceive of him, his is a meaningful story, which is precisely what escapes science. Man's story prompts a question: why is there something rather than nothing? He is the creature who seeks to give meaning to the universe. He does not provide the answer, and yet the quests this question entails are already meaningful. Man is this passing creature who gives a name to the universe. By stammering out a meaning, he gives birth to the universe, which without him would fall back into the torpor of unconsciousness.

We do not know man's being. We only know him through his myth, his fleeting and uncatchable aura. We are therefore forced to remain attentive to this myth, to keep it in view, if we wish to save this creature whose essence is unknown.

The unity of the human species rests upon a common condition. Humans are differentiated from other species not by their biological characteristics, but rather by the particular gaze with which they question the world. Wonder and questioning are what make man, or his tragic apprehension of finiteness. He distinguishes himself by his unique way of inhabiting the earth, one apparent at all times and in all places. The tales of Homer, almost three thousand years removed from us, tell of emotions and worries similar to our own, and this is true of any chronicle from any continent. Tribes without a written language develop forms of wisdom similar to our own. This is very much why we applaud the struggle of Las Casas, who, in the sixteenth century, defended the humanity of the Indians. The way human beings relate to life always makes them living beings, beings thrown into the cold, ever-familiar with life's answerless questions. In this respect, all men are contemporaries in spite of time; and all men, through an awareness of their intrinsic vulnerability, are close to one another in spite of distances.

When a weary culture comes to the point of thinking that nothing can be said about man, out of sheer lassitude in face of all the contradictions or out of revolt against all the determining limitations, it by default destroys the common world of humans. This negation of humanity's constitutive condition can be found at work both in totalitarianism and in postmodern nihilism. If man is no longer distinguishable through his condition, then he joins the ranks of the animal species and dignity disappears as a distinction. There is no unity of the species without its sharing in common a consciousness of its finitude. To endeavor to abolish the boundary between man and beast is to deride the uniquely human faculty of wonder and our awareness of our essential precariousness.

Over the past two centuries man has resembled a dethroned king. He has just realized that his planet is not the center of the world, that he himself arrived late and will disappear early, that the universe did without him before and will do without him again, and finally that there is no biological divide between him and the long chain of consciousless beings. His uncrowning has given rise to self-deprecation: humanity now has doubts about its real superiority. It wonders whether its self-ascribed value might just be a front for its selfishness: the valorization of man becomes "species-ism," a racism of the human species towards the animal species. From then on, if humanity is no longer sacred, everything becomes possible, from hatred to mass assassination. The English eco-warriors, defenders of animal rights, do not hesitate to use the most barbarous and violent methods imaginable against their opponents. Late modernity finds itself in open contradiction with itself when it simultaneously defends human rights and rejects the transcendence of man with respect to nature. The boundary that marks the unity of the human species is not a fact of science but a moral exigency that requires an ontology in order to ensure its permanence.

Perhaps human dignity is just too serious a thing to be left in the hands of men. And perhaps the biblical tale does indeed represent the only guarantee against the temptation to displace the human species. It is nothing more than a story, one might object. Yet dignity does not exist without this story, for dignity was discovered or invented along with it, and all our efforts to establish other foundations have turned out to be very poor substitutes. The creation story, which bestows meaning, guarantees human dignity better than any form of reason ever could. For the problem is not to ensure that human dignity exists: this is the only certitude that we have. We do not need to prove it since we hold it to be above any proof. We need only assure ourselves that it does not rest on arbitrary foundations that any science claiming to be omnipotent or a *sui generis* morality might reconsider at the turn of every century. In this respect, the biblical story of creation, which raises man to the level of God's image, serves less the cause of God than the cause of humanity. To say that man is made in the image of an indescribable God is simply to guarantee the requirement that animates us: we do not want man to be treated as a thing. It is to authenticate the compelling certitude of his stature, to withdraw this authentification from rationalist inquiry. Naturally this guarantee and this authentification then become bound together in a mystery. Yet no science could ever provide us with this guarantee, the only one that really matters to us. For we do not know exactly who man is, but we are sure that respect is owed to him.

Our moral certitude overwhelms and goes beyond our rational knowledge. If our present time no longer accepts this mystery of man in the name of faith, then let it at least accept it for the sake of the proven consequences of its rejection. Let us not believe that we will avoid future tyrannies by endlessly rehashing the memory of past tyrannies. We will do so, rather, by legitimizing the certitudes that can prevent further fragmentation between human groups— whatever factors may lead to it. Feeling remorse and blaming our ancestors will never suffice unless we also reflect on the causes. The repetition of a crime is avoided only by exposing the subterranean foundation that gave rise to it, by undoing its hidden dynamics. The totalitarianisms of the twentieth century are neither metaphysical categories nor maladies of destiny; nor do they mark the sudden appearance of Satan in history. They have human and visible groundings, earthly explanations, the essential explanation being that the nineteenth century rejected the unity of the human species and the idea that its ontological dignity was a mystery beyond the reach of any science. Totalitarianisms are not only moral wrongs, but wrongs perpetrated against a human truth. By not wanting to reject the notion that "everything is possible," we are paving the way for similar abuses today.

Of course, to base human dignity in a mystery does not solve the question of the gray zone or *limites*. We will always ask ourselves whether *homo habilis* was already a human, or at what point exactly an embryo must be considered a human being. The rejection of the *limites* visible at the edges of humanity, the claim that there is a strict boundary between human persons and other living beings, would put us into absurd situations. In the extreme (although the idea of strict boundaries also includes extremes) we would have to prosecute a woman who uses a contraceptive to destroy the first embryonic cell, or mourn to the same degree a deceased relative and a miscarried one-week-old embryo. In this regard, it is easy to see that the discoveries of science have brought these very real *limites* to the fore by erasing the artificial divides of the prescientific age. The reality of the living universe is oblivious to divides between man and animal, potential man (embryo) and full-fledged man, the healthy and the ill. The movements from one to the other category are imperceptible and, at the margins, laws are useless. It is not, however, the reality of these limit zones that gives rise to the dismantling of human unity. It is rather our inability to come to terms with the discovery of these *limites* without calling into question the unity of the species. Human specificity does not depend on science, which can destroy it at will: it rests upon an interior exigency.

Prudential wisdom consists precisely in acting within shadowy areas, where bearings have a tendency to disappear. But prudence is not a form of pragmatism; it is a virtue. It may dispense with overly strict principles on the condition that its eyes remain fixed upon the points of reference that lie above those principles: there is an immense difference between allowing someone to die and decreeing that all the dying who have reached a certain point are no longer persons. Modernity long believed that the development of science would render religions obsolete. In fact the contrary is true. The more this zone of uncertainty between man and animal, embryo and full-fledged human, the ill and the healthy is revealed, the more spiritual criteria become necessary to delineate humanity without ambiguity—at least if we are sure about wanting to guarantee human dignity. For spiritual criteria alone can act as bulwarks against the inescapable consequences of this confusion. Without an ontological foundation, dignity evaporates wherever a gap opens up, whether it be a biological, moral, or mental gap. If we truly want to anchor and maintain the unity of humanity, we will have to admit that man is not only defined by his qualities; he is not simply an animal who holds up a mirror to himself, or an autonomous animal. Otherwise, the dignity of some will cease to exist the minute these qualities are no longer theirs or are no longer specific to them. If dignity is temporary, variable according to age, and liable to disappear and reappear, what then is it really worth? If it depends on the subjective view held by society, how can we consider it irreducible, and how can we prevent a hierarchical sorting of humans in the future?

Temptations to call into question the certitude of human unity appear in every epoch. But every age excludes different human groups: each era succumbs to the idea of establishing the superiority of the group that best reflects the dominant values of the moment. The slaves of antiquity were considered subhuman at a time when the value of liberty legitimized the nascent democracy and republic: the group of "free men" who emerged alongside the unfree had real worth. The Indians of the sixteenth century were treated as subhuman because they were suspected of not having souls, at a time when faith in God was the criterion of excellence. The treatment that was called for by so many writers in the nineteenth century, and then finally inflicted by the Nazis, on the so-called "inferior races" expressed the value placed at that time on biological and "racial" criteria. Under communism those who did not belong to the immaculate class were considered insects. Contemporary eugenics, which begins with the selection of embryos, expresses, as did Swedish sterilization, the exclusive values our society confers upon health, beauty, and bodily and mental normality.

Every era, under the cover of a widely shared value, may try to undermine the certainty of unity and thus become criminal. At the time, all the dominant currents of thought defend this choice, and those who become indignant enter into dissidence, since they reject the consensually predominant value. Who today would dare to challenge the ideology of health, our veneration of the body?

This is why it is essential to identify what new and tortuous shape this old temptation of human selection will take. Today, as a century ago, the blurring of the line between man and animal has desacralized man. Certain currents of thought have decreed the equal dignity of all living beings, even of everything on earth; they thereby construct a "world" common to men, rabbits, and mountains. This, however, is not a world but a place, for a common world is woven out of relations between consciences. In the same vein as this imposture, and quite naturally, there is a growing separation in human society between the more human and the less human—specifically, between the healthy and the ill, the handicapped, and the dying. This separation corresponds, as the previous ones did, to the fears and fantasies of its time: in our case, concerns about the perfection of the body, the achievement of radical well-being, and the freedom of the healthy. A part of humanity could well see itself deprived of human status, cut off from the human world. Those who stand up against this separation are of course treated as backward-looking, since the separation, as usual, is presented as a kind of progress capable of solving a crucial problem. Can we accept "preventive euthanasia," which would guarantee biologically correct children? Our recent history urges us to avoid falling into this trap yet again.

Any selection that separates the more human from the less human—or, to use current terminology, *persons* from *unpersons*—is the consequence of man's control of his self-definition. If we decide to take control of the definition of what it means to be human, to turn it into a possession of ours, to define it according to our historical or ideological whim, then we break man himself. This appropriation of man's definition engenders what we clearly recognize as catastrophes. The obligation of respect forces itself upon our conscience; we do not invent it; it serves as a foundation and is not founded. This obligation includes the unity and specificity of the species, without which it turns against itself: we are not the arbiters of the definition of man. In this regard, we find ourselves in a situation of dependence, at least if we do not wish to reject what clearly seems to us to be what is most worth saving in this culture.

The unity of the human species does not lie within the scope of science. It is a *compelling certainty*. It arises from a self-evident exigency. It compels us unconditionally and forces us to recognize the indispensability of its message. It holds sway through the fear of the consequences its absence would bring. Today, the certitude of human unity is based upon nothing but this fear—a salutary fear, the last refuge of the lost. The certitude of human unity was born in the religious story of creation; it takes root today in the terror-ridden actual experience of its disappearance. At a time when no one can point to an objective Good, this compelling certainty has become the first positive foundation upon which the positive hope for a common post-totalitarian world might be established.

To that end, we must first recover a positive image of man as both person and subject. If one looks for explanations of the mounting antihumanism we see around us, they are to be found in the progressive effacement over the past two centuries of the acknowledgement of man as a free and responsible being. The certitude of respect, which originated in an ontology, has always been a vehicle for a corresponding anthropology: if man is great in value, he must be so by virtue of his independence of mind, his moral conscience, and his engagement in the world.

CHAPTER 3

THE UNALTERABLE HUMAN FORM, OR
THE LESSONS OF THE TWENTIETH CENTURY

Ever since 1989, the year that marks the end of the twentieth century, Western minds have clearly acknowledged the dehumanization at work behind the Wall. Few, however, are willing to describe communism as a self-deception and intellectual imposture. An offense against the good is always accompanied by a rejection of the true, and since Plato, philosophy has known that justice and truth walk hand in hand. If in communism, a wrong was committed against mankind, it is because there was a misinterpretation of what humanity is. The patent failure of communism in every country where it attempted to achieve its goals points out once again that, as far as mankind is concerned, everything is not possible.

We are not yet willing to admit the seriousness of our experiences. That is why we are not able to begin debating the shape of the future world. The end of utopia—the utopia of progress and the utopia of communism—has given rise to almost no reflection at all on the causes. Hence the profound malaise that has accompanied that end. The failure of utopias leaves in its wake the painful realization that we will have to come to terms with a fact revealed to us through catastrophes of epic proportions. "Before our very eyes, "writes Marcel Gauchet, "we have witnessed the death of the revolutionary faith in earthly salvation without really having realized the significance of the fact. Before our very eyes, the possibility of sacralizing history has vanished; for the communist cause died due to the disintegration of what is believable itself—much more than to the contrary evidence inflicted by reality on belief."[1] How, then, did the believable disintegrate from the inside out, if not by the awareness of its radical imposture, of its inability to move beyond words into the realm of life? Yet hoping to save the idea of utopia, and to escape from the daunting task of comparing utopia against reality, we tend to regard the fall of communism with surprise. It is as if no human reason could be sufficient to explain the disaster of so magnificent an idea.

The "contrary evidence inflicted by reality," or rather the knockout punch, is nevertheless there, if one looks, in the dissident literature—the writing of victims whom we respect as victims, aside from our feelings about the philosophical collapse of which they speak. But we scarcely want to know what really happened. This is why our future remains closed and our present turned in upon itself; these are the consequences of a denial fed by two, often related emotions: for the most radical, the desire to save utopia from its association with such a disaster; for others, the fear of discovering the philosophical foundation of the failure of utopia.

It is not enough to have lived through experiences to enter into the future. They must also become the objects of our consideration. They need to be observed, translated, pondered, brought forward with us, so that the future can become more than just the passage of time. Reinhart Koselleck described the experience that is "saturated with reality."[2] To be open to experience means to accept reality: to be honest, which in this case refers to both an intellectual and a moral quality. Honesty consists in looking, which might seem easy, but actually is not. First, to look is to interpret, whereby "reality" is debatable. Second, reality points an accusatory finger at us. It challenges our prejudices and the illusions that grow out of our prejudices. It destabilizes our triumphs, which it can turn into failures. In fact, real bravery is necessary to confront this formidable adversary. We can ignore it, but it always catches up to us.

Intellectual honesty becomes concrete in the courage to change not only our ways but also our theories. Experience means trial. If remembering, as we claim, has become a duty to us, it must nurture reflection as to *why*; without such reflection it remains an open wound, a blindness, useless to the present and future.

Only a free mind can embrace experience because it alone can divest itself of ideological prejudices. It alone can make good use of experience because experience as such does not lead to new certitudes: it closes certitudes and opens up questions. The past century has taught us that looking at the future as if it were a *tabula rasa* is as dangerous as it is ineffective. Our future, as a mere block of time, will continue to be woven out of essential determinations that escape our will. Our future, as a perspective of time that provides meaning, will continue to be woven of cultural determinations without which we could not live.

The force of human catastrophes compels us to meditate upon the obscure weight that sinks utopias: a truth about man that limits the omnipotence of the will in the drive toward perfection. We cannot reshape humanity according to our will. The horror that grips us as we look back upon the spectacle of the twentieth century shows us that a mysterious order has been subverted. The task before us is not to stop denouncing the extermination of human beings and societies—far from it: our task is to trace to its origins the denaturing of human beings that was extermination's call to arms. The obligation to reckon with an incorrect understanding of mankind thus becomes a moral obligation—so long as we admit, having drunk the bitter cup down to its dregs, that utopias sow death. We are limited in what we can realistically hope for. The category of what is possible imposes itself upon us, and our recognition of this fact is the prerequisite for any reconstruction. This prerequisite reduces us, then. It does not tell us to what extent nor how far it reduces us, but at least it forces us to reflect on the impossible, to be mindful of our limits. There is something in the human that endures. If the *new man* of Chernychevsky[3] turns out to be a murderous dream, then the investigation into what man is becomes heavy with meaning.

There will be no post-totalitarian future without a clear and well-argued rejection of everything that built the anti-worlds of the twentieth century. The future will not take shape without the loss of illusions, which are laid to rest only by a clear-minded examination of experience.

To respect man does not mean to respect a concept, but rather a being who has specific needs. To hold man in contempt, as did the totalitarian utopias, is to disdain precisely that which man needs in order to be man. Respect for human rights translates into a respect for human needs that are known to exist; it does not spring from the invention of the human by those who would create worlds to suit their whim. Antiutopian hope is anchored in a human world that is not *invented* but *recognized,* including its needs and dreams, which hope protects and expands. It seeks to recognize and rescue that without which humans perish in despair.

Given all that was attempted in the twentieth century, and the inordinate number of societies that, to their obvious misery, acted as guinea pigs for utopias, to refuse to ask the anthropological question would be downright improper, an expression of contempt for the guinea pigs, in sharp contrast to the moral correctness we constantly profess to have. The history of culture, that whirling record of experience, carries with it experiential knowledge about man. Although the interpretation of such knowledge is always debatable, its pure and simple rejection, the reiterated and overwhelming assertion that it means nothing, is more than just an intellectual error: it spits in the face of history's victims and hurls an insult in the face of the future.

The "utopias" of the twentieth century rested on the myth of self-creation, self-foundation, and on the self-sufficiency of mankind,

conceived to be capable of rebuilding any lost heritage. They claimed
that one could say nothing about mankind, per se. The reexamina-
tion of totalitarianism therefore calls for thinking about limits, which
are statements about mankind. Limits bestow a name and an identity upon man, since the human being takes his name and identity
from what distinguishes and therefore limits him. The lesson of the
twentieth century is the following: we have limits that we do not
choose, and which it would be in our interest to accept rather than
suppress, given the damage attempts at suppression have caused.

Limits express finiteness. In every era the concept of limits comes
from memory, the foundation for an understanding of man as a
natural and cultural being. But the definition of limits is uncertain.
We must always transgress limits in order to make more of what has
been bequeathed to us. The danger, however, is that of profanation.
To transgress is to seek to go beyond limits, to integrate them into
the realm of the possible in order to push back the impossible. To
profane is to violate the deep-seated foundation of the human world
by breaking it apart, including its limits, both present and future. In
silent respect for the human world, we can be zealots of transgression, inhabiting limits in order to make them our own, clearing for-
ests without either destroying or replanting them. For ages, we have
been learning who man is, but we possess neither his definition nor
his redefinition.

The time has come to put an end to experimentation of any kind.
Human matter, which we proclaim must never again be used as can-
non fodder, is also not predestined for the life of a guinea pig in
utopia's cage. The terrible consequences of our self-assured omnipotence should lead us to restore a human world where limits are respected. I am personally relieved to think that the human form is no
longer at the mercy of a few ideologues who are themselves little
inclined to submit to the kind of experimentation they propose. In
general, however, the demise of the utopian demiurge is considered
"unfortunate" ("the greatest of these misfortunes [caused by the death
of communism] is of an anthropological nature; with the dissolu-

tion of communism there also disappears from the human conscience any prospect of the radical political transformation of humanity"),[4] since the primary concern of late modernity remains not to "regress" by restoring to favor the very truths that utopia set out to discard. To recognize the existence of a human form, even with changing contours that must constantly be redefined, to recognize the existence of limits proper to our humanity, would be to move backward, to give up something that had been gained. Many would rather die than take up certain of the old postulates—for example, that of the ineradicability of evil. All kinds of feelings can be discerned in our post-utopian discourse: anger at having been wrong, a desire to save face. Very natural feelings, to be sure. One would hope, though, that they will quickly disappear, at least among those whose job it is to think. For one major idea dominates in this discourse: the certainty, clung to come hell or high water, that man is indeterminate, thus preserving our liberty to do with him what we will. Man must be empty and malleable, capable of becoming anything, so that future experiments will still be possible. Our era would like to preserve this malleability so that the utopian will can survive the collapse of the twentieth century's utopias. Those disappointed by communism still aspire to transform the human world into a field for experimentation: "[T]he world is everything we experiment with until the breaking point . . . , the modern individual, in the experiments he performs on himself, takes the liberty of testing himself to the limits of self-annihilation."[5]

The totalitarian spirit will never really be tamed and vanquished without a return to experience as a necessary corrective to the urge to experiment. These two cognitive processes involve our relationship to reality. Experience embraces the real; experimentation wills to possess the real. Experience has its eyes open; experimentation has a tight grip on things. The European Faustian spirit is constantly moving back and forth between these two poles, the one serving the other, for experience alone would mean blending passively into the world, while experimentation alone would produce mad and manufactured worlds. Only the use of both approaches, each serving the other, makes possible the kind of transgression that is not profanation. Only the recognition of the validity of experience can erect barriers at the edge of the inhuman chasms of experimentation. To experiment is to be closed within oneself and one's own bare will. To experience is to embrace being—but this movement of the mind has left us. It will have to be relearned, like a lost art.

CHAPTER 4
DERISION AND REVOLT

How can the lessons of experience be learned while Western consciousness continues to long for utopia? Modern man thought he saw what Gregory of Nyssa called despairing Beauty,[1] the perfect beauty of the Good, glimpsed in a rare moment, then instantly gone. The loss seems unbearable. The lover takes to wandering a world where nothing pleases him anymore. This is how so many former disciples of communism look, marked as they are by what Central and Eastern Europeans call the "Hegelian bite." A bite is a wound, a tearing of the protective tissue and its penetration by a foreign body that permeates it—with poison? Dogs bite, but so do snakes and scorpions—and then they withdraw, leaving an open wound. Egalitarian utopia undoubtedly represents the most ancient social dream, having been longed for for centuries. Whoever has seen it close up, or believes himself to have touched it, or who has thought himself to be fervently paving the way for its majestic advent, simply cannot get over it. Once the dream is shattered and failure confirmed, the disciple takes to running after its shadow. He calls after it, gropes about in the dark for it, and above all, relentlessly destroys anything he comes across that does not resemble what he is looking for. He is hostage to his old desire, which henceforth has no object. The wound is bleeding and life is draining out. He could bandage the wound and wait for it to heal, bearing the scar as a symbol of mourning for his lost hope. But he would rather die than live deprived of that which the wound reminds him. He begins to hate this world, which has revealed itself to be incapable of achieving the Good. He blocks it out, preferring not to see its mediocrity. Thus can we explain the bitterness, resentment, and rancor harbored by the present era. Resentment consists in spurning reality out of frustration for what one cannot obtain, and the discontented spirit thus bears the mark of self-loathing. The nineteenth-century anarchist, who loved humanity more than anything, believed in the effectiveness of chaos to achieve happiness. Today, the disciple of communism, having been disillusioned, no longer believes in the advent of the Good: he condemns reality out of spite.

Vital resistance and resentment are the two main responses to the events of 1989. Vital resistance: the mind realizes its mistake—it admits, for example, that nationalization of the means of production does not produce a happy society, but rather laziness and constant shortages; it refuses, however, to let go of the idea because of its passionate attachment to it. Existence—adventures, friendships, successes—is nourished and permeated by this belief to such an extent that the belief becomes an identity; the individual cannot renounce it without committing a kind of symbolic suicide. No one can admit, except by entering the circle of wisdom, that his existence reflects the resounding echo of a failure.

Vital resistance frequently becomes intertwined with resentment. The individual is faced with a mistake to which he has devoted his entire life. Having borne witness to it like a martyr, lived according to his erroneous belief, he has suffered, in his own personal history, the catastrophic consequences. It is like the passionate participant in the events of May 1968 who advocated an upbringing and schooling in which nothing is forbidden—one aspect of the utopia of progress—and then later suddenly realizes that his own children obey no creed or law. When his error finally dawns on him, he realizes that it is much too late to change anything: he prefers then to discredit what he does not have rather than to recognize the harmful consequences of his theories. He methodically ridicules any form of education other than his own, pointing out flaws that predictably manifest themselves everywhere, exaggerating the missteps from which no form of behavior is exempt. This logic of resentment, generated by the interplay of self-deception and envy, and magnified by a feeling of undeniable personal responsibility, excludes any pretensions of having been a victim and reveals the presence of a grudge against reality. The widespread ridiculing of traditional rearing and educational practices very often stems from this kind of unspoken unhappiness.

Vital resistance may lead to a split between theory and action within the same individual. Such a person then finds himself sufficiently clear-headed to refuse to suffer the catastrophic consequences of his ideology, but he is too proud to publicly abandon it. He leads an upper-middle-class life, but relentlessly disparages the middle class; he runs things as though he were a free-market advocate, but jeers at free-market ideas; he enrolls his own children in demanding, even austere schools, while preaching indulgence for delinquency in schools attended by the children of others. In other words, he continues to propagate the utopia he no longer lives by, and attacks the moralism of those who simply put into words what he himself is doing. This conscious schizophrenia has something shameful about it, for those who are less cultivated and have less sophisticated minds are the ones who pay the price for this imposture. In this case, the price of saving one's own honor is a diminished life for everyone else. All the while, society is deprived of the benefits it might draw from the lessons of history and remains mired in the harmful habits that experience has long since denounced.

To play down the importance of ideological failures, it is claimed that every reality is—to an equal degree—the product of an ideology. The market economy or the traditional family are thus regarded as abstract systems applied as a veneer over nature and no more adapted to human nature than any utopia. The status of ideology is seen to apply to any political, economic, or social phenomenon or behavior: everything is equally artificial. This move plays down the erring ways of communism by making a return to traditional ways seem like a new folly, one that would be just as inhuman. Underneath lies a certitude assuming the form of a dogma: there is no such thing as human normality, nor are some structures better suited to human needs than others. If this is true, what happened in both recent and ancient history has no more meaning than what did not happen. Events can teach us nothing. The existence of those who preceded us leaves a memory but has no meaningful traces. Every organization is equally artificial, for humans are made of a soft wax, to be shaped by the will of politicians. There is no reality to the human world. Everything, from top to bottom, is a construct, and consequently, everything is still possible.

To date, the countless victims of the communist utopia have left only an embarrassing memory, a troublesome obstacle to persuading anyone to start building new utopias. In this regard, though the accomplices in communist crimes have not managed to hide their deeds, they have managed to strip them of meaning; they have made of them chance events, linked to nothing. Just as our knowledge of Nazism has not persuaded us to erect radical limits to genetic engineering, our knowledge of communism has not persuaded us to place radical limits to social engineering. Our societies tend to think that any experimentation is permissible as long as the instrument of terror is not used: let us aim for the same ends, but with more subtle means. For example, there is no longer any question of outlawing traditional forms of behavior; instead, they are ridiculed with incessant denigration, and their all-too-obvious mediocrity is the subject of sarcasm. In other words, it is a question of destroying by discrediting that which squadrons of henchmen in the service of power were unable to undo.

Communism counted on and hastened the disappearance of religions, but in contemporary democracies religions are disappearing on their own. Communism may have decreed that politics would ultimately disappear, but in today's world civic life is denigrated by citizens who stay away from the polls. Communism did everything it could to break down community and hierarchical bonds, encouraging even family members to inform on one another; these bonds are now undone by indifference. In other words, we have not really broken with this recent past; our world is an extension of it. It is as if the nihilism of late modernity were pursuing the uncompleted work of utopian ideologies.

One can attempt to eliminate religion by exterminating clerics or by destroying churches, but this attempt is generally bound to fail, since fervor grows with persecution. On the other hand, our effectiveness is greatly enhanced if we seek to eliminate religion by ridiculing it, by characterizing it as Neanderthal or by referring to all churches as sects. The same goes for any behavior or institution one wishes to be rid of. History teaches that if terror is unstoppable in the short term, derision achieves the same ends as terror but does so in a more profound way. Leaving outward manifestations intact— monuments, living places, words—it poisons the roots, which brings about the inevitable and durable collapse of these outward manifestations as well. It is true that totalitarianism also made use of sarcasm. But terror itself, while making existence painful or intolerable, confirmed the righteousness of its victims. Tolerance, on the other hand, professed even while engaging in the most acerbic derision, quashes resistance more surely than any outward constraint ever could. The cultural world to be abolished is emptied of its meaning, stripped of the significations that made it both serious and deep and that bound us to it. Derision proceeds by disdain or distance, and through its use the cultural world is neutralized or disarmed, kept from really counting or from defending itself, prevented from offering a meaning by which man might be nourished.

Since the Enlightenment, Western man has lived in the expectation of an earthly salvation—either the progress of Condorcet or the Marxist future. The present world consequently always seems temporary or on the brink of disappearing. So now it is a matter of merely shoving it gently aside entirely, since it is meaningless. With its congenital mediocrity, its tragedies, its heroes, and its gods, the world as context and as a text to be interpreted has lost its significance and remains in our eyes a foreign place. Pierre Boutang spoke of a "declaration of strangeness,"[2] the feeling of the absurd that comes from waking up in the middle of the night, or from the repetition of a word ad nauseum. Thus, Sartre's hero, Roquentin, busies himself with endeavors to deprive the world of its meanings, and this distancing ultimately leaves him free, naked, and shivering.

De-signifying must take place before re-signifying can occur. The past two centuries have tried to replace old structures with other ones in order to put a new face on the human world, and thus advance along the path toward earthly salvation. The hope for salvation, which took the form sometimes of real socialism, sometimes of sacralized progress, employed subversion in order to level the obstacles standing in the way of *the* Revolution. Now that the scales have fallen from our eyes, and the expectation for salvation has been abandoned, a melancholy conclusion forces itself upon us: "Here we are, condemned to live in the world in which we live,"writes François Furet.[3] Nonetheless, the wheel that was set in motion to dismantle meaning keeps on turning.

Derision—the weapon of negation, armed laughter—may correspond to a new project of re-naturing man without the use of terror: everyone will now shape his or her own nature, each of us will invent the existence that suits us best. The postmodern ethic consists in legitimizing experimentation on oneself, on the condition that it is voluntary. In totalitarianism's "everything is possible," which had no recourse other than violence, we think that it is only violence that is dangerous. We must therefore bring about this "everything is possible" through other means. Late modernity still believes that we can do anything we want with man, on the condition that it be done in freedom: the same ideology is still at work, but in a different form. Of course it is true that totalitarianism is monstrous because of the terror it practices, but the root of its error is every bit as frightening: the certitude that, as far as man is concerned, "everything is possible." This certitude is shared by the totalitarian and democratic societies of late modernity alike, for it borrows its source from the religion of progress that gave birth to them all.

For Francis Fukuyama, who foresees a recreational yet meaningful future, "biotechnology will be able to accomplish what radical ideologies of the past, with their unbelievably crude techniques, were unable to accomplish: to bring about a new type of human being." This alteration of human nature will be achieved through genetics and drugs. The massive distribution of Ritalin to turbulent boys and of Prozac to depressed girls will eliminate melancholy in the latter and violence in the former—the main causes of human unhappiness. The genetic revolution will make these transformations hereditary. Is it possible that a posthuman race will come into being along with the end of history? The possibility of such an end "depends on the existence of a human anthropology that is grounded in nature." If science turns out to be able to successfully replace the failed social engineers, then "we will have definitively finished human History because we will have abolished human beings as such. And then a new, posthuman history will begin."[4] In other words, the social and political revolutions having demonstrated, in addition to their madness, their inability to bring a new humanity into being, the achievement of this same goal will be entrusted to the medical or genetic revolution.

The tremendous hope modernity had of bringing about the perfect society, the pure human being, sometimes through totalitarian ideologies, sometimes through uninterrupted progress, left us with the understanding that the incompleteness of man was a defect. Minds acquired the habit of denigrating the mediocrities of the present, as though these mediocrities were somehow only temporary. Once one realizes that nothing perfect will ever be accomplished here on earth, impure reality remains under a curse precisely because it is impure. Late modernity has inherited from Valéry's Faust "exasperation at being a creature." It continues to try to break down that which has always resisted: finitude as the framework for being. It mocks and deconstructs what it has been unable to appropriate.

And so the disappearance of ideologies has left their foundations intact: the primacy of the idea over the real, and the particular bent of mind which persists in disparaging being in favor of an abstract "good." Having been unable to bring about perfect societies that satisfy its thirst for the absolute, the spirit remains locked in its habit of denigration. The postulate by which concrete being is to be denied remains inscribed at the heart of our societies. Our behavior draws on this protest against reality as its source.

Various manifestations of human existence are then disavowed because of the difficulties or abuses that they generate. Love, for example, is readily portrayed in women's magazines as a sort of illness: "it hurts too much," say the models or the stars, who prefer short-term relationships to stressful attachments, as did the heroes in Aldous Huxley's *Brave New World*. In the cult novel by Houellebecq, *Les Particules élémentaires* [Elementary Particles], cloning promises to deliver humanity from the disappointments of sexual relationships. Giving by one person to another is in itself suspect because it is never entirely untainted by selfishness: "He gives," we hear, "but it is only to give himself a clear conscience." We tend to perceive in every behavior only its unwanted effects, because we do not accept the impurity of what is consubstantial with us. And in many cases, we prefer to avoid a feeling, or to reject an institution, rather than to live in the mediocrity that they reflect. Turn-of-the-century individualism feeds on a weariness with the kind of interpersonal relationships that give rise to dependence and quarreling, carry the risk of disappointment, and demand concession and patience. If to bond with another person turns out to be so complex, so imperfect in its unsatisfied hope, then it is better to be alone, free, and without any expectations at all.

We have not accepted finitude as fundamentally structuring man's being. We think we can erase evil by dissuading human beings from adopting behavior patterns that are likely to lead to suffering, or by promoting new institutions designed to sift out everything but the positive: "Le PACS, for better, with no worse."[5]

All the efforts of modern ideologies went into suppressing certain human expressions of life in society that were considered responsible for perversions. Rousseau indicts private property for the inequalities it generates. Marx rejects political power for its constraints. Engels suggests that marriage should be eliminated because it causes jealousy. Thus, the utopian spirit has attempted to rid us of entire facets of human reality, from the yearning for religion to the family and the state, law, and private enterprise. We continue to be suspicious of religion because it generates fanaticism, just as we are suspicious of the market economy because it feeds the selfishness of personal profit-seeking. We cannot tolerate deviances, and would rather defend nothing than defend behavior or institutions prone to abuse. What reasons could we possibly have to cherish this mediocre reality, under the pretext that all attempts to get rid of it have led to moral catastrophes? We accept it with sagging shoulders and heavy hearts, and we hate it all the more because we have not been able to shake it off. We no longer create utopias because horrible experiences have turned us away from them, but our spirit continues to stray beyond the real, ever hoping to escape.

Our hope then is no longer to build, but to destroy. As if it were necessary to do away with being in order to do away with impurity: catharsis once consisted in organized terror against successive groups, but it now consists in casting aside the most demanding forms of behavior. The visible trend is one of slow deprivation, a shrinking of being as the price to be paid for a reduction in evil: a narrow, restrained life lived on the cheap, and the erosion of entire facets of existence. Belief in transcendence, political projects, relationships with others made profound through self-giving and durable through fidelity—all this is slowly withering away out of fear of imperfection and abuse. In its stead is left a vacant and impoverished existence that is both transient and timid. So it is not surprising that a new avatar of Stoicism is flourishing as a response to this shrinkage. This effort consists of resisting the movements of the soul that might trouble it; of seeking immobility without ripples; of ceasing to hope in order to escape the inevitable disappointments. We do not love life. We love only our revolt.

As a consequence, human existence is exalted in a minor mode, in its crude and almost savage aspects; in a morality rooted solely in emotion and the satisfaction at finding out that in this respect we resemble the highest primates; in an obsessive sexuality equated with love; in passionate interest in the various parts of a fragmented body; and in the gradual disappearance, justified on a case-by-case basis, of personal responsibility. These signs of collective psychological regression reveal the emergence of a *Homo silvaticus*, a man anxious to return to a natural, primitive state, to abandon whole sections of a world he cannot manage to accept. The utopian ideologies venerated an abstract man; we venerate a man increasingly reduced to his biology. These two reductions, each in its own way, insult humanity.

Because neither the utopias nor sacralized progress kept their promises, and because they offered, instead of the promised paradise, either snakes or new mediocrities, what is now taking place is a sort of escape into nothingness, a suicidal longing rooted in bitterness. It is better to have nothing at all than to be stuck with the promise of endless imperfection. In the eyes of some, since humanity has fallen from on high, having failed to achieve its demiurgic ambitions, and since it is responsible for unforgivable crimes, it has nothing left to do but to disappear. "How beautiful the earth would be if it were restored to its natural glory," writes the Movement for Voluntary Extinction.[6] How sad it is that the Creator, although aware of his mistake, nonetheless saved Noah. . . . Contemporary man, called *the last man* by Peter Sloterdijk, is "the mystic consumer, the integral user of the world, that is, an individual who does not reproduce, but enjoys himself as if in a final state of evolution." The last man "demands a kind of right to self-extinction. . . . The global process, on the whole, more closely resembles a large-scale party of suicidal individuals than it does an organization of rational beings aiming for self-preservation."[7] Man calls for the right to die, and uses up his existence under the impression that he is the last in his lineage: let us stop here, humanity has lived long enough. In the meantime, he escapes the painful reality and the boredom of an era without ambitions, which explains the use of drugs viewed as an individual right, trance-inducing music, or rave parties, in which "it is not a question of creating a counter-culture but of producing a counter-reality."[8]

It is very much in social and interpersonal life that our difficulties and suffering arise—"hell is other people." And so the individual who enjoys a solo existence can congratulate himself for having avoided the worst. The young raver begins a solitary dance in the midst of a mass of dancers who are identical and separated, each of whom finds refuge in inward ecstasy. In the altered state produced by drugs or trance, questions are no longer asked. In solitary life, shared reality, which involves relationships with others and questions about meaning, becomes distant. The solitary individual confines himself to his basic needs, for it is the face of the other that throws questions at him like so many daggers. To escape these torments, he drains his life of meaning and voluntarily lowers himself.

Through an inept but constantly repeated comparison between the radiant future and the world as it actually is, modern ideologies ended up hating the latter, guilty as it was of resisting the march of progress. Compared with the radiant future, the present seemed ultimately negligible and worthless: this is very much why totalitarian states were able to perpetrate the "assassination of the present" prophesied by Alexander Herzen in the nineteenth century. Today, the debacle of the attempts to create utopia has left this hatred for the present world intact. Totalitarianism hated reality because it no longer had any meaning in relation to its expectations. We hate it because it no longer has any meaning in and of itself.

More precisely, the ideologies that claimed to respect humanity and to work for its good, loved in humanity only its reinvented image. Just as the church during the Inquisition loved only heavenly man, communism loved only future man. It did not respect man, but cherished a superman, an image without existence. This is why it was so dismissive of the fragile and incomplete being who inhabits the earth and wrote him off as a loss. The ideologue had contempt for the present and treated his contemporaries, at least those he had not already eliminated, like cattle only just good enough to roll out the carpet before the future: they were the proletariat chained to the Plan, or "the Aryan race" condemned to reproduce like so many racehorses.

Late modernity no longer knows which man to hope for. In fact, it no longer expects anyone. It only knows that it still hates imperfect mankind, which no power has been able to replace. But any genuine humanism must love this incomplete being as an ineradicable inhabitant of history.

CHAPTER 5
THE TRACES OF A WOUNDED ANIMAL

The dissidents of the Soviet bloc, especially in Central Europe, have analyzed the meaning of their struggle with precision and depth, and through them comes to us a plea to safeguard the world of being.

What is the meaning of their struggle? They struggled against a power structure, supported by official and secret police, against a ruling caste, and against a certain form of despotism—and so they appear to have been freedom fighters. But that is nothing. Or rather, it is only the tip of the iceberg, the political consequence of a philosophical situation that extends infinitely beyond it. The dissidents struggled much more against the will to make man live in a way that is not his, to re-create him in a way he cannot be; they struggled against the systematic destruction of man's reality.

Western public opinion has not understood a thing when it considers Havel or Walesa to be simple descendants of the first Brutus: their aim was not only to dethrone a tyrannical power and to liberate speech and political, educational, and economic activity; they were concerned with reestablishing the rights of man as he actually is. The combat of the dissident is philosophical because beyond tyrannical politics lies a human truth that was crushed and rejected.

This is why the revolutions of 1989 aimed to restore being to its true place.

The Marxist ambition to reinvent man established a separation between the world *before* and the world *after*. The separation naturally turned out to be brutal, since it was, after all, a question of fabricating a new species. Entry into the new world was to occur through a sort of asceticism that was at once personal and social. In this process, each individual was to rid himself of the old man within. Each was to struggle against the temptation to return to the safe haven of received ideas. The communist makes himself out to be a man of the open seas: he burns his bridges behind him and rushes headlong into the absolutely new.

The dissident says that he wants to save what remains of these bridges. He regards this debris as "tracks,"[1] or "traces." The question is why he wishes to rescue a world that has almost disappeared, a world that our era has consciously tried to erase. This might look like the pathetic nostalgia of someone who cannot stop mourning the past, like the attachment to the old-fashioned that characterizes reactionaries, who are actually on the same side as the communists: the former point to oldness as the absolute criterion of the good, the latter to newness. But for the dissident, the yardstick of *when* something happened is of no importance. The "good" is that which suits man, that which makes him happy.

In Kundera's short story, "Edward and God,"[2] the hero is accused by his colleagues of going to church: how could a young man believe in God? Edward acknowledges all the theoretical reasons for abandoning belief in God: faith is a vestige, it takes us back to prehistoric times, it is not worthy of the new humanity. However, he shamefacedly says, "'I recognize that faith in God will lead us to obscurantism. I recognize that it would be better if He didn't exist. But when here inside I . . .' he pointed with his finger to his heart, 'feel that He exists . . .'" And a colleague concludes, "The struggle between the old and the new goes on not only between classes, but also within each individual man. Just such a struggle is going on inside our comrade here. With his reason he knows, but feeling pulls him back. We must help our comrade in this struggle, so that reason may triumph."

In Bulgaria in the 1950s, for the great feast of Orthodox Easter the regime did not actually close the churches but rather allowed only old women to go in. A little boy who had accompanied his grandmother came out of the church with a candle in his hand and was beaten by the police in the street. The older women were confirming the order of the past. The little boy was committing an offense against the future.

Whether it makes itself manifest through Sovietism or in contemporary democracies, the ideology of progress always expresses a rejection of, even an accusation against, humanity, fallen from its throne because of "backwardness of conscience" or "mental immaturity." What is called "maturity" here is a purely rational age, as defined by elite opinion: "In periods of maturity it is the duty and the function of the opposition to appeal to the masses. In periods of mental immaturity, only demagogues invoke the 'higher judgment of the people.'"[3] In the France of the 1990s, objective and respectful mention was made of a survey indicating the indulgence the French showed toward soft drugs, but if a majority were to call for a return to capital punishment, the mood would turn to indignation over the reactionary character of our compatriots. Majority rule has its limits under an ideology of progress *sui generis*, as dictated by politically correct opinion, that functions as though it were an enlightened elite. What does the development of social maturity mean anyway, and with respect to what points of reference? "Questions of personal pride; prejudices such as exist everywhere against certain forms of self-abasement; personal feelings of tiredness, disgust, and shame—are to be cut off root and branch."[4] It means, wrote Koestler, that man is to be torn away from his narrow world where he finds attention, remorse, and forgiveness. Today this would probably translate into tearing man away from his guilty past, from his heteronomous beliefs, from his backward behavior patterns of respect and trueness to himself. In either case, it means tearing down the meanings by which man establishes his bearings, finds his identity, and engages his future.

If it is indeed possible to speak of the development of individual conscience in history, it is nevertheless inappropriate to think of this development as a movement from childhood to adulthood. Soviet man and the individual of late modernity play a character who has exited history, the role of an invented mature adult. Neither is an adult in this sense. Nothing allows us to believe that they are free of prejudices; they simply re-create other prejudices. Each, in his own way, lives on the sidelines of life. The ideology of progress equates happiness with "maturity," or replaces happiness with "maturity" as a criterion of the good. Maturity means a distancing from childhood. The more society differentiates itself from the past, the better it will be.

Dissidence is devoted to preserving human unity over time. It refuses to relegate our predecessors to the shadows of the past, to the realm of "societies in their infancy." It believes that they participate in the same condition as do we. In reality, it is possible that although they are dead, they are also more alive than we are. It is possible that in order to distance ourselves from them, we have buried ourselves alive. What binds us to them are the "traces."

These "traces," or vestiges, are nocturnal remains, aspects of man's dependence. The dissident seeks to rescue a truth about man, the kind of truth from which man is entirely liberated only at the cost of self-destruction. That is how the persistence, even the obstinate survival, of these traces, these remnants, is explained. They are what is left of reality when one attempts to dismantle it, and manages then only to live in an unreal world: "Reality is a wounded animal that drags itself around in search of a place to hide, leaving behind a trail of blood."[5] The trail is what lingers of the truth, if what one means by truth is consistency with present and living reality, not consistency with a supposed future reality. "The dissident," writes Predrag Matvejevic, "is a hostage of truth."[6] The dissident volunteers to keep watch over this exposed and threatened truth, to remain vigilant so that it does not entirely disappear.

The world of the Soviets and the world of the West both have their roots in the sacralization of progress, or in the certitude according to which the sole criterion of the good is liberation from previously held beliefs. The France of today would concur with the reproach Edward's colleagues in communist Bohemia levelled at him: how indeed can a young man possibly do something like go to church? A large number of reforms are rationalized as progress defined in terms of liberation. Those who dissociate progress and the good, who suggest that progress be judged in light of the good and not the contrary, are accused of being reactionaries. In other words, to better society is increasingly to extract man from his habitat, to disentangle him from all the networks of meaning that imprison and shape him. But this process alienates him. Like totalitarian ones, Western societies also attempt, and for the very same reasons, methodically to reconstruct cultural reality. But in order to do this, they use derision instead of terror, which is merely another way of practicing exclusion. As a replacement for physical constraint, verbal contempt is an extreme measure, one that marks the uninterrupted continuation of hatred.

The conscious will to nullify the religious question and keep man apart from God was solemnly proclaimed in the Universal Declaration of Human Rights of 1948. The Preamble states: "Whereas disregard and contempt for human rights have resulted in barbarous acts which have outraged the conscience of mankind, and the advent of a world in which human beings shall enjoy freedom of speech and belief and freedom from fear and want has been proclaimed as the highest aspiration of the common people. . . ." Thus, in an authoritarian fashion and by decree, the highest aspiration to which we can lay claim was assigned to the temporal realm. The heavens were closed by magistrate's order! The term "proclaimed" indicates officiality, ultimately in a comical way since it is rather difficult to decree an aspiration. We know that the declaration was written with a view to universality and owes much of its shape to concessions made to the Soviet regime, which never did sign it. Nevertheless, since 1989 no attempt has been made to rework this proclamation—on this point or on any other.[7]

Social aspirations are not everything there is to humanity. Today we live in a truncated world. To treat lightly grave questions, those which weigh heavily upon existence, is to show contempt for the human beings who ask them. Religious questions cannot be rubbed out like punctuation errors. They are our heritage, they characterize and differentiate us: "The absolute cannot be eradicated, it can only be degraded."[8] To deprive humanity of a dimension of existence, whether it be religious, moral, or aesthetic, amounts to an abduction of being—a philosophical crime even if it is no longer a political one. He who is made uneasy by questions of good and evil becomes neither a noble savage nor a neutral and colorless being, for such a being does not exist: any passing cruelty, if it is the least bit persuasive or appealing, attaches itself to his amorphous conscience and conquers it. He who no longer sees the necessity of discerning the boundary separating truth from falsehood will not take on the peaceful countenance of a newborn child but will rather be receptive to every passing bit of nonsense, willing to believe the assertions of any guru. The abduction of being is a violent story in which we have perhaps not yet witnessed the worst chapter.

Nietzsche described the great questions about which humanity wondered as illusions. In fact it is the will to deny them that has turned out to be an illusion. In a wild maelstrom of irrationality, late modernity simultaneously derides spirituality and bemoans the triumph of materialism, proclaims moral relativism and becomes indignant over the spread of pedophilia, claims that all is in vain and deplores a society where boredom can lead to suicide. Every society expresses what it has been given. Even though they are always debatable, answers to the eternal questions of mankind are all that can raise barriers, however fragile, against the chaos of meaninglessness. One might argue that our answers will be insufficient and prone to pretension, or that suffering will reappear along with hope. Supervielle, speaking of human faces, described them as being "awkwardly immortal." Seeking to avoid, out of pride, the label "awkwardly," modernity preferred to abandon religious questions altogether. The inhabitants of late modernity need to reconnect with their humanity.

Many ways of being and thinking, say the dissidents, have been decreed old-fashioned and yet have survived in secret. It is possible that these remnants represent in fact an imposing proportion of the structures of existence, even though we view them as old foolishness, or as foolishness because they are old. It is possible, too, that they are not mere residue that the winds of history are destined to erode, but structures without which we could not live.

Of course, these pesky remnants remind us of our dependence, but to forbid their recognition would be to accept a lesser way of being. It is true that, in a way, man is alienated from the very habitat that nourishes him. Yet can one deprive him of it for that reason and then call such deprivation alienation? Am I alienated by that which enables me to live? Dissidence emphasizes two aspects of this underground world which obstinately resists all attempts at systematic eradication: prejudice and scruples.

Prejudice takes root in specific times and places and reflects an era's genealogies of thought. Prejudice has often lost its justification through overuse, long use, and habituation. Modernity hunts down prejudice, often for good reason, because it is a conduit for errors that have never been challenged. Modernity detests prejudice to the point that it seeks a kind of crystal-clear reasoning, based on pure objectivity. Ultimately it demands a form of reasoning that for man is unattainable. For what is human thought stripped of the impressions, moods, and passions that history leaves in its wake like so many layers of sediment? Kundera's hero describes belief in God as a feeling. "No one has ever yet proved that God exists," insists his interlocutor. Indeed. This prejudice nevertheless forces itself upon the character's mind like a kind of extension of the self, its inner structure, and the atmosphere in which the self thrives. It is easy to see the danger prejudice poses. But what should also be seen is the danger of a life without a history, a life deprived of its unfounded fears, its secret venerations, and its indescribable superstitions. A man who was able to know the world by objective reason alone would be deprived of any personal ways of thinking: modernity depersonalizes by rationalizing. To want to rescue prejudice, therefore, does not mean to defend obscurantism, but rather to defend the shadowy side of man that makes of him an individual being through his complex relationships to time and to inner and outer events.

It is quite possible that what is most important for us is precisely what cannot be proved: for example, the intrinsic dignity of every human being. This paradox becomes clearly visible when the rational systems of modernity give rise to acts that we cannot help but see as human catastrophes. This tendency leads us to take up the defense of scruples (from the Latin *scrupulous,* or little pebble), which bother the moral conscience like pebbles lodged in a shoe. Such doubts about the rightness of an action to be undertaken reveal the difficulty of embodying moral precepts in concrete existence. They may, as is true in the case in point, represent the last remnants of conscience after customary or historical morality has been, or is about to be, thrown out the window. Scruples are what resists the will to transform or destroy morality. They show up in the writings of Darwin and the first advocates of eugenics at the end of the nineteenth century: basic reason, they say, would have us not prolong or even destroy the lives of "undesirables," and yet our scruples keep us from doing so; thus, civilization is rushing toward its ruin.[9] Scruples here rest on no clear foundation, the thinking of the time rejects them, and social analysis demolishes them. They represent a tiny and contemptible obstacle to grandiose undertakings. But it is precisely these seemingly insignificant objections which must be listened to, for they are bearers of the meaning—albeit sometimes unfathomable and irrational—of our common existence. The one who sweeps away our last scruples, the one who presides over the auto-da-fe of scruples, is Hitler.

Today we are inundated with reasons to go ahead with human cloning and to create genetically perfect children; we are restrained from indulging these ambitions solely by scruples, which stand in the way with all the insolence of a pebble in a shoe. Any ninth-grade student could come up with the necessary arguments to junk these scruples, which grate upon the conscience and paralyze it without any serious reason, since they come from a morality we are determined to reshape according to our needs. These bothersome remnants are perhaps more than just remainders of an ancient world to be eradicated: they are perhaps the ultimate and persistent traces of a human truth that we rashly wish to efface.

The untiring defense of these traces, which are visible in prejudices and scruples, is in no way similar to defending traditional values or tradition as a value. Although the defense of these traces does claim that the future is not necessarily better with respect to the idea of progress, it does not claim that the past was necessarily better either. That question is beyond this debate. In this regard, the defense offered by the dissident contests not progress, but rather the ideology of progress. It wishes to put its finger on what deserves to endure, because there are things the absence of which is much worse than their presence. Defending these traces can only be undertaken at a time of decisive *tabula rasa*. It is when human existence has been thrown into complete disarray that the ineffaceable becomes fully visible.

Just what are these traces of? What is the foundation that has been destroyed, that was or still is under attack, but that we need in order to live? If the question is complex and controversial, it is first of all because the question itself contains two questions that are too often thought to be identical. The first concerns anthropology: what is man, and what are the limits beyond which we begin to destroy him as such? The second concerns cultural anthropology: what are the cultural referents that Western man cannot forgo except by losing what he himself defines as his own identity?

The twentieth century went so far in its questioning of foundational values and human limitations that it attempted to strip European man entirely of both. And in fact this is still going on. It is as if, in the process of dismantling our cultural edifice, the twentieth century could not be content with merely attacking its foundations, but had to attack the very ground on which this culture, like all others, rests.

The vertigo of self re-creation even goes so far as to deny, for example, that humans are inevitably sexed beings, and, consequently, that there is a complementarity between the two genders, man and woman: the open subversion of this norm prevents any properly anthropological discussion of the issue.[10] This ultimately represents a radical rejection of human finiteness, if it is true that sexuality expresses our fundamental insufficiency as a need for the other, which is described in all our myths of origin: the eternal God of the Bible does not create a laborer and a poet, but a man and a woman; the pride of the hermaphrodites, who believed themselves to be self-sufficient, writes Plato, led Zeus to cut them in half.[11] In various forms, this pretension to self-sufficiency oozes from every pore of late modernity.

Nonetheless, our relentless self-questioning focuses on, above all else, the essential reference points of European culture; it is no longer a matter of anthropology, but of cultural anthropology, even if the boundary remains difficult to establish. In this questioning, the sometimes clear and sometimes implicit intention is to challenge not only the human condition in general, but certain essential foundations of our culture. Within that framework, the scruple of which the dissidents speak arises in opposition not to human beings as they might be, but in opposition to Western human beings as they wish to be. We can indeed cast aside entire categories of our cultural referents, but at what cost? In this abandonment, will we remain conscious, thinking beings—the persons-as-subjects whose contours are outlined by our culture? Do we really want to reject this figure, the subjective self? This is the real question. As humans, we are structured by our awareness of finiteness. As Europeans, we live in a cultural world structured by the figure of the person-subject. Insofar as they are being contested, these two interlocking worlds call for justification.

CHAPTER 6

INSUFFICIENCY AND THE HUMAN WORLD

It is possible to speak of a human world if we recognize that humans are connected to one another across space and time by the questions that gnaw at them. Contrary to the animals, we cannot take life for granted: this is why man has an existence, and not merely life. Scientists tend to call the great apes human as of the time they began to ritually bury their dead. From that point on, they pose disquieting questions about death and, in response, murmur man's intuition of transcendence: what is there in him that makes him able to conceive of a universe that does not conceive of him?

It is possible to speak of the emergence of different cultures as architectures of specific answers, ever-vacillating and groping, offered up by different groups in response to the questions that are the mark of humanness.

These disquieting questions express the awareness of insufficiency: man is the animal who has become aware of his precariousness, and who, for the first time, has realized that he is a passenger on earth, that he inhabits a world in which he never fully belongs. The construction of a cultural world is related to this disquiet and sense of inadequacy. To constitute a world is not only to live together, in a group, band, or collectivity, for the purpose of better satisfying basic need; even more, it is to weave together coherent meanings that allow us to exist on earth as wayfarers capable of speaking about ourselves. The wound of the finite being who knows himself to be finite thrusts him toward common speech and action, gradually giving rise to a world. Human beings invent or discover gods, rites, and laws in order to inhabit the earth from which their awareness of finiteness has, so to speak, dislodged them. The cultural world becomes a dwelling place that offers shelter for their troubled spirits.

At another level, political organization finds its legitimacy in a similar way. Aristotle, the first theoretician of European "politics," cites the concept of insufficiency in explaining how the family and the city came into being. Man and woman "cannot exist without one another,"[1] because each one alone would not be able to "leave behind him a being like himself."[2] The political community is organized in order to make up for what the individual lacks: the emergence of conscience, which brings man out of animality, makes laws, myths, and norms necessary, because without them man becomes worse than an animal. In other words, man is engaged in a flight into the future: he cannot dream of a return to the brute nature from which he has emerged, for his awareness of his tragic situation in the universe keeps him from doing so. He must either produce a cultural world or become a barbarian. Thus, the greatest danger for him from this point onward is to deny his own finiteness: "He who is without a polis by reason of his own and not of some accident, is either a poor sort of being, or a being higher than man."[3]

Since World War II, an obsession with "civilized barbarity" has reigned in Europe. It is a legitimate obsession, and if certain ecological currents of thought prefer animals to man, it is because, in the course of the twentieth century, man revealed himself to be more cruel than animals. What has been forgotten is that man becomes civilized through the cultural architecture of myths, norms, and laws. Totalitarianism made humanity barbarous by depriving humans of their cultural world. Nazism uprooted the foundation of the culture of dignity by rejecting the unity of the human species; communism rejected the expressions of this culture without replacing them—law and morality are bourgeois, hence to be eliminated. It arrived at barbarity through the annihilation of properly human requirements, for a society without laws and morality ends up forgetting the very foundations of its humanity and therefore treats some men like animals.

It was another rejection of culture—well-intentioned, to all appearances, because spontaneous and peace-oriented—that inspired the sociological upheaval of May 1968, only to generate directly the violence we now see in our schools. A cultural transformation in relationships involving authority was necessary in the 1960s, if only because of the democratization of higher education. Yet something is truly transformed only when it has been replaced, and our generation merely created a void ("It is forbidden to forbid"), leaving the door open to barbarity. And this very same generation today, alarmed at what it refuses to recognize as the fruit of its errors, has reached the point of demanding a police presence in the schools. Human beings become civilized by acquiring a *sum-bolos*, which alone repels the *dia-bolos*. The latter, expressing separation, violence, and hatred, is countered only by symbols that form bonds, that weave together authority and interdiction—in other words, that which is said (*-diction*) between (*inter-*) us. When a government honors the group NTM,[4] the destroyed symbol of motherhood leaves in its wake a dizzying vacuum for barbarity to fill. We may have rejected totalitarian terrorism; we have not restored the common world that its postulates destroyed.

If every cultural world responds to the insufficiency of man by offering him answers to the questions of existence or by giving meaning to his anxiety, the answers offered by each cultural world are nonetheless fragmentary, and in a way, relative. No culture can claim to be universal in actuality, nor to have discovered the pure truth, capable of solving all human problems. This characteristic—that culture is inevitably incomplete, that every culture is a rough draft—has contributed to a revolt against culture itself in the modern West.

The illusion of perfection leads us to reject our own answers, which are considered to be too narrow: if a norm holds only on this side of the Pyrenees, we might just as well do without norms at all.

The emergence of the *individual,* supposedly freed from the culture that weighed on him, reflects a false sense of sufficiency: the individual believes himself to be the source of both the questions and the answers, to contain within himself the alpha and the omega, and to provide himself with his own points of reference. He wishes to bind himself to others only through a voluntary contract, a contract he can nullify if he no longer wishes to be a party to it. In other words, he rejects the bonds that preceded him and any debt to which he has not agreed.

If the individual believes himself to be sufficient and wishes to be a world unto himself, he then believes that he no longer needs any cultural world, or rather that his cultural world is represented by behavior patterns, ideas, and definitions that he invents the moment he needs them—and rejects as soon as he considers them obsolete.

The contemporary individual has many basic needs that he cannot fulfill by himself, though: political society supports him anonymously by providing him with whatever financial support and services are owed him. And so he believes that he is self-sufficient, not that he can procure everything he needs to live, but that society makes up for his deficiencies out of fairness, automatically. He then is tied to the welfare state by an umbilical cord that ensures his subsistence, and yet considers himself to be essentially self-sufficient. The individual is no longer really aware of his own finiteness, or else considers it to be a holdover from the past. He is impatient to be delivered from his various dependencies—sexual, marital, social— in order to achieve in life the completeness for which he believes he has the potential.

The contemporary common world finds itself torn apart not by the violence of combat between divergent answers (as was the case with the religious wars of yesterday), but by each individual's withdrawal from the questions that are the mark of humanness. More profoundly, each individual withdraws from questioning itself. Communism destroyed the common world in order to make man self-sufficient, to keep him from being dependent on laws, myths, and institutions. The man of late modernity discards his cultural world because he believes himself to be independent, to owe nothing to anyone, and to have been released from inherited obligations. The presumption of self-sufficiency keeps him from building a common world, since such a world structures itself around an assumed finiteness. For I cannot defend the postulates of a common culture unless I accept the ever-uncertain nature of human truths. The purpose of these postulates is not to spare me anxiety but to make this anxiety meaningful. I can neither give nor receive if I do not know my own deficiencies. I can only forgive if I know myself to be capable of evil. The contemporary individual neither gives nor forgives; nor does he acknowledge any common truth, because he believes himself to be in a position of autarky.

Man's awareness and admission of his finiteness as a tragic wound place him in a precarious cosmic condition. His maladjustment defines him: he wants what he does not have and does not possess what he wants, he wants immortality and always dies, he wants goodness and does evil. The very strangeness of all this makes him a being about whom something can be said. About God, we can say nothing. Man fashions common cultural worlds that attempt to speak about man.

The very term *condition* signifies that man does not escape all determination. He is not a free agent; he carries ballast. The contemporary individual believes he is capable of inventing whatever it is he wants to be, and takes himself for God. In this respect he has inherited that ideology which thought it could reinvent humanity, cast off the ballast of constraints, and play the demi-urge. Contemporary individualism represents the continuation, in solitary form, of the utopian dream.

The first thing one can say about humanity concerns the existence of a certain *condition*. This condition can be recognized only by leaving behind the same theory of domination that constituted the foundation of Marxism and still inspires the present epoch. The past two centuries acquired the habit of explaining constraining human characteristics, or determinations, as the result of oppression orchestrated invisibly by a dominant group: thus, the capitalists are held responsible for the necessity of economics, and the bourgeoisie for the need for politics. The notion of a plot undertaken by a given dominant group or class, aiming to express their selfish demands in the form of an irreducible "condition," marked the heyday of the utopias. Today, for the defenders of gay rights, it is the "systems of domination and oppression"[5] emanating from a social order that falsely persuade us that the heterosexual norm is tied to nature. And for the militants of cultural deconstruction, Dead White European Males are responsible for the domination of both women and colonized peoples, giving rise to a culture of repression that must be combated.

The utopias found their legitimacy in the postulate that human determinations were brought about at some point in history through the agency of malevolent interests. This scapegoating no longer makes sense after totalitarianism. There is no historical plot against such and such a group. Rousseau's or Engels's miserable man who invented private property and selfishness never existed. No one ever tried to taint the excellence of the Germans, who, wrote Fichte, had not been affected by original sin. The dominant classes who govern the state use necessary mechanisms: they may appropriate the state to their own ends or corrupt it, but they do not invent it. No group with questionable motives is perpetuating the heterosexual norm to safeguard its own power. The white male has concocted no conspiracy against women or against native peoples. There is no capitalist machination against mankind to keep it in misery. In other words, Zeus as portrayed in the myth of Prometheus, jealous of his power and wishing to keep hidden from humans the doors of their liberation, does not exist on this earth. Economic, political, and sexual determinations are borne by each of us like so many disquieting questions. Every cultural world carries within it the temptations of domination. Every necessary authority can become oppressive. As a finite and free being, man is always a hair's breadth away from perversion, and his creations are laden with mines. Recognizing that we are shaped by a *condition* is like being diagnosed with a congenital and incurable disease. Actually admitting it is so terrible that we invent boasts and fallacious arguments and bend over backwards to relieve our distraught minds.

The person who has just learned that he has an incurable disease can refuse to face up to the diagnosis and go into various forms of denial. He thereby enters a process of permanent revolt, for the effects of the disease always catch him by surprise and seem to him to be undeserved injustices, or else he enters into a process of perpetual lying, for he will have to constantly provide himself with false reasons for his ill-being. If, on the other hand, he faces up to this misfortune along with all the rest, if he analyzes it and comes to terms with it, and if he makes a place for it in his life without seeing in it some evil design or injustice, he can achieve a new happiness—one enhanced by the struggle he has waged with himself.

Similarly, to perceive man as a determinate being reveals an open wound in the flank of existence. A wound must be tended, for fear of even greater misfortune. Existence becomes structured around it, and no one can exempt himself from it. We are not independent from our condition, in the sense that a person suffering from an incurable disease cannot throw off his disease, discarding it like a superficial attribute. Totalitarian utopias were similar in this sense to the sorcerer who drives out an evil spirit from his patient's body and confines it within an object.

The wound of finiteness is precisely what establishes the human person as worthy of dignity. Man is great not because he has resolved his questions but because he has to come to terms with them. He is great in this tragedy, through his conscious finiteness. The ignorance of animals is twofold: they do not know that they do not know. Man's conscious vulnerability, in contrast, compels respect. Dignity is what compensates for the weakness of this vulnerable creature, thereby reestablishing his greatness.

Just as Descartes' subject knows that he exists because he is conscious of his doubt, a person knows his true stature because he conceives of himself as wounded. This is undoubtedly why the contemporary individual, elevated by his pretension to self-sufficiency, is skeptical of humanism and instead values the animal world. Man as the demiurge of the self no longer needs anything. He fulfils himself. From this standpoint, it is the baby seal that, in comparison, seems so vulnerable and demanding of respect.

Only by recognizing his essential condition can man achieve the fullness of his being. Nothing truly makes sense beyond the reality of this wound, unless one engages in illusion and delusion. He who rejects this preexisting given in order to invent himself loses his human form and loses himself. He may destroy, but he invents nothing apart from monstrous figures—justified precisely by the fact that he does not believe in the "monster" as defined by a certain vision of "normality."

A common cultural world is nothing more nor less than an appropriation of the human constitution—a specific translation or judgment of what it is to be human. Thus the norms of a given time and place build upon the essential determinate traits of the human condition: by nature man is a sexed being; by culture, he institutes the matriarchal or patriarchal family.

Late modernity rejects these various natural and cultural determinations, either because it still clings to the utopian idea that humanity has no inherent shape, or because it rejects previous cultural models because they are all relative. This is why late modernity inhabits no world.

In this respect, reappropriation of the human condition would entail giving up the possible for the sake of being, giving up indeterminate potential for the sake of real action. Much contemporary thought, which follows utopian logic, prefers liberty to determinateness, which invariably closes doors. I can become anything if I say that I am nothing definite. The absence of hope is a product of this very indeterminateness: one cannot hope for nothingness; one can only hope for something definite, for a projection of being. To hope would be further to deny myself something I do not hope for. The potential of the contemporary individual remains intact, replete with all possibilities, but empty of being. The example of the indecisive person or of the aesthete becomes a compelling model—an ardent anti-model. Indeterminateness consists in the desire to explore, to refrain from making choices, or rather to choose the possible over the real, the likely over the true, well-being over the good, the moment over time. Total liberty is ambitious but without declared ambition. Indeterminateness provides a great euphoria, an illusion of plurality and perfection. It offers refuge from a reality that is hurtful and hurting because it is incomplete. It reflects a singular ethic: the indeterminate individual asks that he be judged by his intentions, and that he be measured only by his possibilities.

The contemporary individual, who can say nothing about himself, is a context without a text. The great temptation of the adolescent is to cling to liberty itself, pure form without content: the pages of Gide's *Nourritures terrestres*[*Fruits of the Earth*] are pages from adolescence. To dare to be something is to take a big risk.

To affirm that man has a definite shape is to allow his possibilities to decrease as being comes into focus. It is to abandon the goal of complete liberty and to affirm one's responsibilities, along with the duty henceforth to protect and defend what is. The spirit divests itself of some of its potentialities by replacing them with actions. It thereby becomes more or less sedentary, ceasing to explore freely. In contrast to the great euphoria of the possible, the weight of determinate being seems heavy indeed. The constrained man is engaged in existence. He has revealed his finiteness and incorporated it into his own time horizon, and having done so, he bears the stamp of his actions: only in this way does he exist.

The presence of the human condition makes it difficult to believe in a "nature" in the sense meant by Rousseau, who described a human being saved from animality but not yet tainted by cultural perversions. The virgin human being that Rousseau described in relation to the history of the world, or the virgin human being that Sartre described in relation to personal existence, does not exist. He is a figment of the philosopher's imagination. As soon as man leaves behind the status of animal, he takes on a unique condition. And it is through appropriation of this condition that he becomes human. From now on, his existence unfolds on an intimate stage, the décor of which he has not chosen. He is not born a blank slate, but is stamped with a double mark: that of his condition as a being aware of his finiteness, and that of his culture, which aims to give a particular and partial meaning to this finiteness—to make it, so to speak, inhabitable.

Because the cultural world and the essential human condition are interlocked—the former establishing answers to shed light on the latter—the task of child-rearing and education involves integrating the child into a *world*. Because the child is oriented by his condition of finite being from birth, he must seek his place within a structure of answers that make sense of his finiteness. This is not to say that these answers must remain immutable and be handed down intact from generation to generation. But the questioning, evolution, and the transformation of these answers can come only from minds that are at once already immersed in the world and able to distance themselves from it. One cannot distance oneself from something that does not already exist. The myth of the child as a blank slate who should not be taught anything if he is to be allowed to make his own choices is an invention of the utopians.

Late modernity, in the lineage of Rousseau, continues to believe that the child is a pure being in whom "society," an almost magical scapegoat, inculcates evil penchants through its alienating cultural referents. The de-referenced child of our violent schools is thus deprived of the common cultural world—deliberately so, thanks to the ideas of 1968, the proponents of which are now in power. The child experiences his existence as a tragedy, which is the mark of his humanness. But he no longer finds around him any answers to his anxieties. Unaware of what can be said about the human tragedy and how it might be tamed, he suffers the full force of its blow and responds with violence to the silence of a society that is reluctant to "impose" on him any particular, thus ever-debatable, answers. By breaking the everyday objects he finds around him, and by twisting the meanings of words, the child *realizes*— shows the reality of—the human tragedy, to which the adults do not have the courage to give meaning. The utopia of the generation of 1968—any given meaning is relative, therefore impure, therefore to be gotten rid of—has produced children who will *realize* the chaos they have inherited. In all likelihood, the coming decades will be brutal and deadly.

The lost meanings are symbols and beliefs, the accessories of our cultural debt. The undefined individual loses form and clings to his material self, a biological body inhabited by instincts and desires. He focuses on his body, which he cares for, redesigns, and coddles immoderately in its individual parts, because the image of the body as a single entity requires a structure of meanings that has been lost. The fractured body described in women's magazines is a sign of regression to a preliterate age that existed prior to our recognition of a cultural world. The man without such a world loses himself: because identity requires interconnected terms, one does not identify with oneself but with a figure other than oneself. The slogan "be yourself" has only relative meaning, then. It recalls a time when society was so communal, so possessive, that the individual had to distance himself from it in order to become a subject. Those times are long gone. In our society of derision, what is urgently needed instead are serious forms, or determinations able to anchor the drifting individual. It is absurd to want to "be oneself" without determinations.

Autonomy does not consist in eradicating determinations on the pretext that they are varied and changing, but in reconstituting them for oneself, selecting those which are important to us, and deciding their relative importance. The uniqueness of each being is forged in the encounter between consciousness and multiple determinations, in the interplay between distance and recognition through which the self is formed. No one becomes a subject without having internalized the world and stepped back from it, in part so that the self can exist. The place of the subject is not invented in a vacuum; rather, the subject shuffles around the bric-a-brac of existing things to make a place for itself among and against them. Education in a vacuum refuses to bring in content from the outside: let us not influence the child. Later in life he will choose his religion or his irreligion, his social and political certitudes. Through a slow withdrawal and a spiral of disengagement, the individual detaches himself from a world in which derision runs rampant: he either feels permanently estranged from it or becomes a disciple of the first passing inanity.

The individual who takes part in the world and who finds nourishment in external meanings by making the effort to ponder them is then able to live as a subject. He needs a world to be a part of and to identify with, a world where even his errors can find meaning.

Because we doubt our points of reference, we hesitate to pass them on to others, or do so *sotto voce*, at arm's length, and half-heartedly. In this way, we underestimate the importance of child-rearing and education and fail to comply with its requirements—more out of derision of its content than out of natural laziness. What's the use in teaching a child such fleeting things, relative to time and place, and finally so doubtful? But the child cannot come to terms with his finiteness if he is not given content, an interpretation, which will never be anything but fleeting and unstable. Our universal condition as finite beings is illuminated only by specific responses. To "raise" a child, in its most concrete sense, is to help him emerge from the naked and unspoken tragedy into which his birth has thrown him, and to give his wound a meaning. Of course, this meaning will be incomplete and always too meager, but it will make of him an upright being in spite of the tragedy and the wound.

Man does not appear all at once when he comes out of his mother's womb. The slow process of humanization is pursued through the care provided at the earliest stages of existence, that is, through child-rearing and education. Men are not made without this slow construction. That is why, under certain dictatorships, kinship communities sacrifice the most elementary needs in order secretly to ensure the education of the next generation (the underground classrooms in Poland and Romania come to mind here). Their stubbornness has as its end less the preservation of a particular culture than the preservation of humanization itself. One need only consider the situation of Russian young people, which is similar to the situation of many of our own high school students: the society of late modernity, believing that early childhood should be wide-open and untamed, creates barbarians.[6] Man is born twice. For him, there is no day without a morning, which is to say, without a childhood forged on the anvil of culture. This first birth, at the dawn of existence, is accomplished through patience and fervor: the adults must be believers and even evangelists of their culture in order to transmit its soul. Every culture is imperfect and has its share of perversion. Traditions are all destined to be challenged. Everything is provisional in the long term. In the short term, however, the provisional is necessary so that the second birth can take place. A society does not have the right to make of its children the guinea pigs of its doubts. A mediocre upbringing is better than none at all. If the chain breaks at any moment, or a link gives way, then a whole society is soon tempted into barbarity—which, instead of nature, is the real flip side of culture. If a child is not born a second time, he fails the promise of his first birth, thereby distorting the nature of that birth by not carrying it to fulfillment.

This second birth consists in the construction of the personal identity that finiteness requires. Man is too insufficient to exist by himself; he must *identify* with a culture in order to express his humanity.

CHAPTER 7

MUST THE SUBJECT BE SAVED?

In *The Origin of the Family, Private Property, and the State* (1884), Engels drew from the work of the American ethnologist Lewis H. Morgan in order to emphasize that the earliest forms of the family were polygamous and polyandrous, and that the married pair appeared late in history. Ancient societies were characterized by both group marriage and collective property. Marriage came into being at the same time as private property and is an expression of male domination. Engels—and the Marxism that followed in his footsteps—justified the abolition of the bourgeois family because of its alienating nature. But he went further: he justified the possibility of this abolition by establishing that this form of family life had been preceded in history by other forms, which could therefore reappear.

Today's debates about the different forms the family can take are based on the same idea. The work of the ethnologist Cai Hua on the Na in China[1] describes a contemporary matriarchal society in the province of Yaunnan in which the "system of visits," a sexual system that is both polygamous and polyandrous, is prevalent. The author's conclusion speaks volumes, "Marriage can no longer be considered the only possible institutionalized mode of sexual behavior. Without marriage a society can maintain itself perfectly well and function as well as any other."[2] Furthermore, "the Na case attests to the fact that marriage and the family can no longer be considered universal, neither logically nor historically."[3]

The similarity in reasoning, a century and a half apart, reflects the continuation of modern hopes: in order to prove that it is possible to radically transform social and behavioral structures, ways of life that are distant in time or place are cited as evidence. If group marriage or polygamy/polyandry have existed before or exist elsewhere, this demonstrates that the institution of the traditional European family is of only relative interest and could just as well be cast aside. The family does not represent a basic building block of humanity nor does owe its form to "human nature"—certainly no more than does private property, if one considers the proven existence of collective ownership in many ancient societies.

Here, a question of cultural anthropology is raised. It should be differentiated from the properly anthropological question—Can man change his sexed nature?—which is raised by the rejection of sexual determination (often expressed in discussions of homosexuality and the right of homosexual couples to have children). The problem posed by modernity is not, Can man live without European-style marriage and family? or, Can man live without private property? Obviously he can, and this has been confirmed historically and geographically. The problem is, Do we really want to take the radical step of pursuing this type of society? What would the consequences be? And more profoundly, would this type of society still maintain the cultural referents that we defend?

In 1999, during a colloquium on the idea of motherhood, one of the speakers noted with great satisfaction a new milestone: for the first time in history, she said, women control procreation and the fate of the embryos they carry, free of social constraints and male domination. This joyous declaration, however, revealed a complete ignorance of history: in many ancient Indo-European societies, let alone in other civilizations, family structures were matrilineal or matriarchal or both at once, and the women had power over procreation and abortion through their knowledge of plants passed from mother to daughter. The case of the present-day Na, in which the man is no more than a "waterer," according to the term used, and in which fatherhood does not exist, is frequently paralleled in primitive societies. The main characteristics of the matriarchal model are the absence of marriage, control over fertility by the mother, the supplanting of the father, and the sacralization of pleasure.[4] An objective look at our society shows that we are in the process of moving toward this model.

Like the passage from individual property ownership to collective property ownership under communism, the present eradication of fatherhood to make way for a modern form of matriarchy is happening in the name of progress. The law of 1999 that created a civil union with the financial and fiscal advantages of marriage, but without the long-term responsibilities, guarantees the predominant role of the mother, the only certain anchor of the filial relationship if the father is not legally recognized in his role. This reform grants additional freedom to adults, who are released from their responsibilities toward their children and toward their spouses; it is thus presented as another step in the march of progress. (In the discussion of this bill in the National Assembly during the sessions of October 12 and 13, 1999, the proponents rested their argument on the idea of progress— "progress of civilization," "dynamic of progress," "advance," "on the side of progress," etc.; adversaries were charged with being "backward-looking.") Nevertheless, this change constitutes rather a return to ancient forms before the appearance of the patrilineal and patriarchal model, just as communist collectivization was a revolution in the direction of well-known primitive economic and social forms that had existed before or elsewhere (for example, among the Incas).

What is important is not the moment in history when these social forms emerged or took hold, but what is driving this return to the cultural past. The collectivization of the means of production and exchange made its appearance in the twentieth century, only to end up as a tremendous regression to a phase of civilization in which personal autonomy and individual freedom to act and think did not yet exist. When Marx learned of the ancient political model called "Asian despotism," he understood that in the past there had been societies in which neither private property nor social classes really existed, and that they were invariably governed by a despotic state. In Marx's time, Bakunin and Proudhon were already predicting that a communist society would inevitably become a modern form of these ancient autocracies—which indeed very quickly occurred after 1917; Lenin himself admitted this at the end of his life.[5]

The conservatives who fear developments that they believe will ignore indelible aspects of the human condition would gain by attending to history and geography before they claim to know what mankind is, for the forms that the human enterprise has taken are sometimes more varied than they might think. But the followers of progress would also do well to learn their own history and geography before legitimizing and legalizing any social development, for the forms of human existence are more coherent than they think, and they risk reestablishing archetypes that contradict their own points of reference. While ruminating in disarray over the problem of "Asian despotism," Marx put his finger on the insurmountable difficulty of coherence. Socialism could not bring about collectivism without destroying the forms of political and individual liberty that a long history had built up. And if European socialism ultimately abandoned its program of revolution, it is because that revolution necessarily involved giving up our most cherished cultural referents, especially the autonomy of the human subject, which we view as the foundation for the subject's dignity. One might well wonder today if we can establish the matriarchal family without discarding personal autonomy and responsibility, which we otherwise proclaim to be essential.

Must we consider this social evolution, which draws us little by little toward the ancient matriarchies, to be progress? It is on the basis of the criterion of the referents we hold dear that we can evaluate what constitutes "progress" and "regression."

In the French context, the evolution toward matriarchy involves not only the family sphere, but the political sphere as well. The republic plays the role of a mother, a dispenser of goods according to the criterion of equality. The citizen of the welfare state situates himself within the symbolism of all-powerful desire, for which the state is the monopolistic intercessor. He is like the child who goes to his mother to obtain any object he desires: if she does not give in, he stamps his feet and plays the victim; if something bad happens to him, he thinks that it is her fault and that she is responsible. While the father is word and law, the mother is place, a spatial dimension that stands between the subject and the outside world. The same can be said of the welfare state, from which the citizen demands everything, with no limit other than the law of desire, and from which he demands an equal share, like the child who demands an equal share of love under the reign of his mother. Under totalitarianism, the state is an evil godmother, a terrifying mother figure, but a mother figure nonetheless. The French republic, resembling Sovietism in certain aspects, such as the national education system, gently reduces its subjects to the level of children.

In this respect, our democracy finds itself at a decisive moment of choice. It must determine whether it will develop a welfare state and matriarchies, giving priority to the individual, or whether it will conserve the notion of personhood through a more liberal economy and family institutions that integrate the responsibility of the subject. A cleavage, albeit a hesitant one, is developing between Anglo-Saxon societies and countries like France and Sweden on this issue. The fate of the culture of personal autonomy is very much at stake here.

Can personal autonomy be shaped in the land of desire? The subject is not a given of nature. The person constructs himself as subject by recognizing the hard law of reality on his own. In order to do this, he needs to integrate the category of the possible with full awareness of what he is doing. For it is only after recognizing what is possible that he becomes capable of making choices. The subject who has been taught to take initiative receives the law from his father and from surrogate authorities so that he can then forge his own law: he becomes autonomous. Man does not become an autonomous person unless he internalizes a law, unless he is willing to conceive of limits by himself, even if he must constantly grope to determine where they lie exactly. In other words, personal autonomy is built on awareness of and responsibility for limits: one gives oneself one's own laws solely in the hope of coming to terms with one's own finiteness, which one no longer wishes to leave in the hands of others, like the child living in the land of the all-powerful mother. A human being can become human only by sacrificing the pleasure principle in order to live within the reality of his own restrictions. If through his upbringing and education he does not come to recognize limits, he will not free himself from the category of the impossible, nor from his own limits: this is within no one's power. On the contrary, he will have to suffer the law of reality, which will now impose itself upon him from without: forced conformity to community norms in holistic societies. Matriarchal society—like a society based on collective ownership, which history shows often went hand in hand with ancient matriarchal society—has no place for personal autonomy. It functions according to the twofold logic of protection and submission—a logic in which autonomy is absent.

Our contemporaries are thrilled to see the solidarity that develops in blended families and support the emergence of "tribal" ways of living that, as replacements for the traditional family, diminish the fear of rising individualism. But if it is true that contemporary tribes do indeed reestablish a sort of togetherness in which solidarity has a part, they could almost never play the role that our culture assigns to the family: the development of autonomous subjects through roles of authority. Recent proposals to give minors the right to abortions or morning-after pills do indeed offer additional individual liberties, giving the illusion that the individual will thus be more in line with the image we have of man. In fact, the opposite is true, for the underage child, who has not yet learned to make choices, will in effect have regulated behavior imposed on her by state authorities. As proof of this, the main argument of those who support these measures is that parents might not give good advice to their daughters: What if an authoritarian father forces his under-aged daughter to keep her child? What if the parents are too negligent to talk about birth control in time? So, out of fear of parental neglect or fear that families might not be conforming to the certitudes of the times, the family's educational role is taken away and given to the state. The child may at first feel that she has been freed from her parents thanks to a law administered by an anonymous authority that hides its ideology under the mantle of science and technology. But in reality, she has lost what would make her a subject. Social agencies may be able to dictate a pattern of behavior, but they are unable to teach autonomy. Training a child to become autonomous is a task that requires mutual trust and understanding, affection, and patience; it is accomplished through trial and error and it entails an acceptance of risk. Only a family in which roles of authority are shared and durable is able to assume this risk. Only a family can offer an education in *initiative*, which is essential to the formation of the subject. The state can offer no more than an *initiation*.

These few examples allow us to understand why the autonomous person is on the wane in late modernity. The capacity for initiative and responsibility, which defines the modern subject, depends entirely on learning communities beginning with the family. Such communities thus form a buffer between the individual and social agencies. But precisely this intermediary barrier gives rise to revolt: to the extent that the family is organized around hierarchies and roles, it favors forms of domination considered unacceptable with respect to equality. Late modernity is not unaware that the survival of the autonomous subject is very much a function of family upbringing. All the same, the figure of the despotic father, of whom Kafka painted an unforgettable portrait, is cited as justification for letting the subject disappear. "The crisis of the subject is on the whole a beneficial disintegration of philosophical maleness and the male theological fantasies in as much as they were rooted in a paternalistic personalism."[6] In other words, the disappearance of the free subject is welcome because the subject can only come into being at the price of familial oppression and, in particular, paternal oppression. Reprising a frequent historical process, European patriarchal organization has invited its own demise by engaging in pathetic abuses. The overly long refusal to allow women, considered as persons, to accede to the status of autonomous subject, carries enormous weight in today's defense of matriarchy. We are perhaps witnessing the systematic destruction of personal autonomy as the only means to quash, along with it, male domination.

The disappearance of paternal authority, however, or of the father himself, will not make authority in general disappear; nor will it spare the individual from oppressive forces. For the individual will after all need a law, and the state will impose it upon him from on high. Once he ceases to accept parental authority, he will fall under the authority of anonymous agencies. This second authority will be different from the first: state law will fall directly, armed with its official power, on the neck of the defenseless individual. Parental law has some chance, with due care, of aiming for an education in freedom, one which will produce a subject capable of independence of spirit in the face of any and all powers.

The experiment of Marxism, which in order to destroy the bourgeois state does not abolish state authority as it claims, but rather gives rise to despotic oppression, seems to have been for naught. The issue is to choose not between submission and total liberty, which does not exist, but instead to choose between submission to a social authority and apprenticeship in a difficult freedom under the tutelage of intermediate authorities that could become tyrannical. This higher and more difficult road obviously makes no sense if we believe like Nietzsche that the subject is no more than a "grammatical formula."[7] It does makes sense if we believe that the subject is an anthropological figure through which European modernity can better respond to the tragic aspect of existence, and which undergirds modern Europe's certitude of human dignity. Rather than dreaming of producing an individual freed from all constraint, the goal of late modernity, at least if it considers the survival of the subject essential, should be to domesticate parental authority by giving parents the means to raise their children to be autonomous. The irresponsible individual who lives for the moment is nothing more than a figment of the imagination, in the sense that he would never be able to survive. Without realizing it, he would need a despot who would force him to reestablish the limits that he himself would be unable to define.

No human society can persist in the face of the chaos of individual capriciousness. In the old communitarian societies, the harmony between rights and duties followed the rhythm of and was imposed by custom. What might seem to be great freedom was actually closer in nature to that of a child allowed to frolic in his playpen: the Na of China take and leave their sexual partners as they please, but within a system of strict rules that govern living together for the protection of children and the perpetuation of the tribe. Under Pol Pot, a mother could legally refuse to feed her children because that was the state's responsibility. When our democracies legitimize the idea that couples have no duties toward their children, we can see in this only a contrivance of intellectuals that leads to reliance on the tutorial hand of the state. The social violence of today stems from, among other things, this situation: the subject, having been "liberated" from his responsibilities, has not yet been placed under the tutelage of political authorities. Into this enormous vacuum rush all kinds of violent behavior. If the human being is irresponsible, he must be brought under control; if he wishes to be free, he must be responsible for the consequences of his acts.

The effacement of the subject reflects a terrible fear of the consequences that might result from the failure of totalitarianism: the triumphant return of the old communitarian societies. In these societies, called *holistic*, the liberty afforded by autonomy does not yet exist. The individual person is both constrained and protected by the group to which he belongs. It would therefore be better, goes the reasoning, to give the subject over to the state, accepting his official abolition in advance, so that he will not be diminished by the group: a sort of preventive suicide—as if late modernity had made the failure of modernity official and destroyed its work for not having been able to bring it to perfection.

The work of modernity has been to make manifest the human person's qualities as subject. Yet this does not presuppose the advent of liberty as a creation of essence—the advent of a subject who changes his nature to become a god. Rather, it presupposes liberty as a creation of existence—the advent of a subject who takes responsibility for his integrity over time and for his identity in relation to the world. The subject remains indebted to the learning process that shaped him in such a way that he may assume responsibility. He does not invent himself in opposition to his communities; rather, through them, he learns to judge them.

Fundamentally, the demanding reality from which the contemporary individual seeks to detach himself is his own insufficiency. The human being who lived in ancient societies knew very well that he could never be self-sufficient. His world gave him laws, took care of him, and recognized him in his role. The major error of late modernity is to believe that the way of progress is the way of individual self-sufficiency. In this sense, it is still drawing from the utopian wellspring. To leave ideological utopias behind would mean to recognize more clearly man's constitutive insufficiency. Then the way of progress would be the way of expanding individual responsibility. The problem for the modern subject is not to achieve greater independence by erasing his own finiteness, but to better come to terms with his finiteness and that of others by deliberately involving himself in his world.

The subject is he who opens his eyes to human weakness and organizes society in a way that responds to this reality. Instead of unconsciously assimilating his heritage like man in olden societies, and instead of rejecting his heritage like the contemporary individual, he recognizes that he is an heir. Instead of remaining submerged in his world like man in olden societies, and instead of rejecting his world like the contemporary individual, he engages himself in this world. Engagement and the recognition of one's heritage are expressions of accepted finiteness even within the quest for freedom.

The modern European culture that invented the autonomous subject stems from an ambitious intuition: it thinks that each human can exist as a coherent entity, holding within the self its principles and dreams.

This is a cultural certitude, the validity of which is not self-evident. But this personal coherence very much constitutes the pillar of Western culture. When considered from the inward point of view, it could be called faithfulness to oneself.

In an instant of thought and doubt, Descartes grasped the unquestionable aspect of the thinking subject. A flash of insight such as his has the feel of certainty, but it is fleeting and unsettled. The existence of a permanent *self* throughout the voyage of life is more a matter of faith than of certainty. I know with certainty that I think and doubt, that I am a subject the moment I think. But I have faith in my identity from one era to the next; I believe that I am the same throughout this whole journey; I believe that I exist as a constant being over time. The thinking subject is a certitude. The personal subject is based on trust, on faithfulness to oneself. The subject never stops experiencing this faith—nourishing it, testing it, overcoming doubts. Through this whole process he makes himself into a coherent being. And it is because he is a coherent entity that he wishes to perpetuate himself through children and cultural works. On the other hand, the human being of ancient societies perpetuated the species through himself, whereas the contemporary individual no longer sees any reason to perpetuate himself at all, since he is neither a branch of the species nor truly coherent.

The Na man is a passing lover and an adopted father (in fact, an uncle), only to end as an anonymous and often abandoned old man once his sister's children no longer want him in their lives. To persevere in a sentiment of mutual love is for the Na a kind of harmful possessiveness, and for the contemporary individual, a danger to be avoided.

Any form of coherence entails renunciation because it cannot tolerate contradiction. It is shaken by imposture. It is nourished by memory. The subject who is faithful to himself lives his history. The ephemeral individual renounces nothing. His own history remains foreign to him: he admits to living successive lives. The contemporary individual, even as an adult, remains an unstable adolescent characterized by his scattered desires, his contradictory opinions, his obliviousness, his irresponsibility, and his constant clamoring for things he has done nothing to deserve but to which he feels entitled. In fact this is why he has such low self-esteem. To the extent that there has to be a minimum of coherence before self-love is possible, how can we reckon with something that is essentially shapeless? The man of holistic societies existed as a member of a group. The contemporary individual is no longer part of an existing group, but neither has he become a self. His mirror reflects no image.

Today, a return to a kind of subjection is taking place, this time not through terror but with the tacit agreement of a lobotomized subject, whose contempt for his cultural world has deprived him of a self. This evolution has two related sources: the growth of individualism, which rejects personal responsibility and seeks licentious freedom; and the entrenchment of egalitarian ideology, for which the responsible freedom of the subject generates undesirable differences. Contemporary subjection is expressed in characteristic and recognizable ways: conformity to official thinking, which treats criticism as an insult to be eradicated; child-rearing and education transferred little by little from the family to the state (and the taking charge by social authorities of the individual, who is now regarded as a ward of social agencies, the family having failed to teach a sense of responsibility); the democratization of opinion; and a belief in collective guilt. At the same time, the philosophical underpinnings of these phenomena are taking hold through the legitimization of ancient and foreign ways of thinking that value society to the detriment of the autonomous subject.

Human rights thinking, which increasingly has the ring of incantation, should question its premises and purposes. If such thinking is truly to be the guarantor of personal dignity, can the societies that advocate it afford to lose the autonomous subject, who is responsible for his actions and faithful to the integrity of his being?

Must the personal subject be saved? This is less an issue of ideological choice than of coherence. If uniqueness is lost, the dignity of the human being in his uniqueness would be lost along with it.

CHAPTER 8
THE MODERN SUBJECT, OR INCOMPLETE CERTITUDES

Born along with the modern development and expression of self-knowledge, the subject responded to a desire to make more concretely real the personal freedom that Europe had always nurtured. At the end of the Renaissance, and at the beginning of the modern era, the subject made his appearance as the one who takes the question of meaning in hand, and by doing so, internalizes the tragic dimension in which the struggle for meaning takes place. In previous societies, meaning was given, conferred externally. With the advent of the subject, the self attempted to appropriate meaning by standing back from the cultural world. Criticizing that world thus became possible. In the seventeenth century, Comenius challenged the idea of education as initiation, fostering instead the notion of education as initiative—the *humanities*, which opened the way for the freedom to think. The person was worth more than knowledge; the person was about to become a subject.

The invention of the subject was an extraordinary venture, but modern arrogance brought it to ruin. The modern subject believed he was a demiurge. Endowed with autonomy, or the ability to make his own laws, he thought he was independent of any law. As a subject, he lost all the certainty of any communal shelter, and the contradictions of existence were thrown right in his face. He used his power to try to suppress these contradictions, an undertaking that ended in failure. Having been unable to re-create himself, he now prefers to deny that he is a subject. But there is something childish in this extreme attitude of all or nothing.

The ideologies of the twentieth century tell the tale of the downfall of this man-demiurge. After having been decreed capable of re-creating himself during the revolutionary period, the subject caught a chill in the drafty air of this adventure. Frightened by the greatness attributed to him, he begged for mercy and asked for protection. François Furet is right when he says that fascism and socialism have their origin, in part, in the difficulty the subject has in assuming his autonomy, in emerging from the old organic society.[1] When each person is faced with the necessity of reinventing everything, the weight of existence becomes just too heavy a burden to carry. When the inner contradictions and wanderings become unbearable, it can be tempting to dispense with questioning altogether. The ideologies of the twentieth century provided supposedly definitive answers for a subject tired of living in perpetual questioning. They were supposed to heal modern man, sick of the unlimited freedom that had been falsely attributed to him. Perverse systems are the result of a misunderstanding of what freedom is.

Nonetheless, the disappearance of ideologies at the end of the century has solved nothing in itself. Now that they are gone, contemporary man finds himself once again alone with his thought and his vertigo. In fact, he misunderstood the meaning of modernity and the personal freedom it ensured: the rise of modern liberty not only promised liberation but also warned of heightened responsibility. What this presaged was not the possibility of freedom from contingency and finiteness, but the honor of facing up to them within a cultural world that is to be kept at a distance but not rejected. This is very much the challenge of late modernity, to which the recent past has not been able to rise, and to which the future must respond.

The contemporary era struggles to reconstitute a common world built this time on personal freedom. Previous societies stood on the firm ground of an existential truth provided to individuals from birth. Modern societies cannot re-create a common world unless they found themselves on a new relationship between the subject and certainty.

Neither form of society engendered thus far by modernity—the ideological society of totalitarianism or the individualist society of the contemporary West—has fashioned an autonomous *I*, free to think and act. They have produced, instead, an individual still subjected either to the orthodoxy of terrorist systems or the weight of an insidiously imposed Good. Under communist regimes it was forbidden to say one was not a communist; in democratic society it is impossible to contest politically correct opinion.

The totalitarian societies of the twentieth century revealed *antiworlds*, in which the life of man was deliberately smothered under the weight of a demiurgic will to change human nature. But contemporary Western societies, committed to the dismantling of common values, are shaping *nonworlds*. What makes the analogy work is a mixture of relativism and dogmatism. Truths are at once changing and rendered absolute: a paradoxical superimposition of the cynic and self-appointed righter of wrongs—someone who engages in constant derision, devaluing everything, but at the same time decrees what is good and what is true with inspired self-assurance. The individual lost in the crowd swings between indifference to all certitudes and submission to received opinion, which bespeaks a deteriorated relationship to truth. Why this paradox? The individual has no certainties, merely opinions with no grounding outside his subjective point of view. He is therefore constantly aware of the fragility of his own thought; he finds reassurance by adhering to dominant opinion. The objectivity of the Good has been replaced by the magnitude of consensus.[2] At the same time, since there is no one to call it into question, dominant opinion feeds on itself. Fortified by its pseudo-certainties, it amplifies them through repetition, like a snowball rolling down a hill. And this is how it becomes fanatical. Relativism and fanaticism are the two dramatically contrary aspects of modernity gone astray. What we really stand in need of is both certainty and tolerance.

The Enlightenment, in spite of its promise, did not establish a new autonomy. It only replaced one imposed dogma with another: the individual who had to call himself Christian during the Christian era in order to conform to common thinking must today for the same reason assent to a certain interpretation of human rights. It is striking to see to what extent late modernity has reestablished precisely the type of society that the Enlightenment intended to overthrow: a society with a single voice, in which the adversary is difference itself. The analogy is troubling. The Christians during the time of the Crusades considered pagans the objective agents of Evil—and we regard the Serbs in the same way. In other words, contrary to what we say, we have not dispensed with received truths; we have merely replaced the contents. This submission reveals the difficulty the contemporary subject has in understanding that moral truth is always a matter of reflection and debate. The modern subject has not yet been born. He will exist when, for example, we are finally able to hold a real debate about whether there can be a just war, or when we are prepared to exercise self-restraint once decisions are made instead of acting like plenipotentiary defenders of truth wherever we go.

Communist "brainwashing" aimed to deprive the individual of his ability to reflect in order to keep him within the closed circle of dogma. In Aldous Huxley's *Brave New World*, the dogma of the future, a sort of ideology of health, is repeated ad nauseum, even during sleep. It is well known that all the dictators of the twentieth century made use of mob psychology and political propaganda; they were experts in the art of keeping individuals under the sway of official views. Today, the brainwashing is carried out by constantly repeating politically correct viewpoints throughout the mass media, a tack taken by governments of every kind. It is odd that dominant opinion should attack religious sects so virulently, for it accomplishes the same domination of thought as do they, complete with threats to possible dissidents—and it does so with the weight of a whole society. This insidious constraint works very effectively. Advanced democracy, said Tocqueville, does not forbid books of criticism, but "has taken away the very thought of publishing them."[3]

The absence of freedom of thought can be recognized by the particular way in which adversaries are identified. They are systematically described as being backward or idiots—that is, as unable to think differently, if in fact they can be said to think at all. When, for example, a deadly bomb exploded in France on April 20, 2000, the suspected Breton separatists were identified in the press as "imbeciles, idiots, cretins." In other words, any conviction other than the approved one is not really a conviction at all; it is just a sign of mental deficiency. Only the approved, dominant opinion can claim to give meaning to its thought and actions. Adversaries are not thrown into prison but are described as making no sense. When a dominant opinion is no longer able to counter other opinions through genuine debate, and when, in addition, it has at its disposal the means to crush its adversaries by casting scorn on them, then it rapidly becomes monopolistic. It thenceforth reigns uncontested over the youngest and weakest minds while it reduces all others to silence. In fact, once this happens, we are no longer dealing with opinion—which by definition entails controversy—but with fanaticism.

So far, the freedom from old dogmas has not given rise to independence of mind, but to alienation from other dogmas. For two centuries, we might say, modernity has been groping its way. It has not yet fulfilled its promises. It would be the honor of the twenty-first century to work towards bringing into being the genuinely autonomous subject, capable of finding his identity by simultaneously rejecting both relativism and dogmatism.

Thomas Mann described the young fascists of his time as lined up in closed ranks under a common banner and ceasing to be subjects, as having relinquished control over their personal selves. They "are unaware of culture in its highest and deepest sense. They do not know what it means to work toward oneself. They no longer know anything about individual responsibility, and find all their satisfaction in collective life. . . . A facility that leads to the worst of lapses. This generation desires nothing more than to take leave of its own selfhood. . . . The ideologies it clings to, like *the State, socialism, the greatness of the fatherland,* are in no way essential to it: They are merely pretexts. The only goal is euphoria; one must rid oneself of one's self, one's own thought, of morality and of reason in general."[4] This was the message: to seek to free the subject from his questions, to try to supplant the disquieting expectations that shape the identity of the autonomous subject, is nothing but an abduction of being, a denaturing of humanity. It is the equivalent of a lobotomy, or of drugging someone in order to deprive him of his faculties.

The fundamentalists of any religion lend themselves to the same kind of abdication of the self. Mann called these human shadows the "new Huns." Time has passed since Mann's era. The subject he had hoped might appear, able to "work toward himself," has not yet been born, except perhaps quietly, without fanfare, among the central European dissidents of the anticommunist resistance. Western societies rightly condemned Mann's new Huns, but they have nonetheless failed to foster the emergence of a genuine subject. For the humanism that stood up to the century's totalitarian regimes was occupied exclusively with dismantling things, with overthrowing points of reference, so that further fanaticisms might be prevented. In the process, it produced an individual who flees himself in a different way. His schools are scarcely interested in developing the conscience, nor in forging responsible or civilized minds, but are devoted more to anchoring the child even further in the society of the spectacular—the "open school"—that is, in flight from the self. Mann shuddered when he observed the fascist youth; he would have felt the same way reading about the various acts of school violence today. Our societies are producing a new generation of Huns, not through ideology but through nihilism. In both cases, a process of depersonalization is at work.

In his personal notes, Eugene Ionesco wrote that he based *La Cantatrice chauve* [*The Bald Soprano*] on a textbook for learning English.[5] The famous play is, from start to finish, woven out of completely vacuous statements of the obvious, from "the ceiling is above us" to "the country is quieter than the big city." It is precisely this superfluousness which makes it funny. Yet Ionesco did not intend to write a comic play. When he was learning English, he thought that the author of the textbook had drawn the sentences from ordinary social banter, a discovery that left him horrified. Later, he admitted having felt embarrassed when he saw audiences laugh at the play's succession of truisms.

The vacuousness of the truisms conveys the emptiness of the characters, who are given the most ordinary names, that is, names that represent citizen X of the United Kingdom—just as they could represent the citizen of France or anywhere else. The characters of *The Bald Soprano* are devoid of an inner life. "They no longer know how to be; they can *become* anyone or anything because, in not being, they are like everyone else—the world of the impersonal—and they are interchangeable."[6] But haven't we tried, historically, to distinguish each being so that he could actualize his autonomy? Didn't modernity seek to liberate every being from the virtual cloning effect characteristic of communitarian societies so that, for us, personal dignity is achieved in society when subjects are placed first? Wasn't it this increased status of the personal subject that Erasmus sought when he praised religious tolerance, that Comenius sought in advocating universal education, and that Locke sought when he defended political liberalism? The alignment of the contemporary individual into neat rows, his dissolution in communal thought, seems to reflect a nostalgia for ancient organicism—for the society of common consciousness in which, as Hegel said, all cats are gray.

We would be wrong to see Ionesco as a typical Romanian—possessor of a dark and sarcastic mind. He was above all someone deeply concerned about late modernity: why has this century done so much to reduce beings to nothingness, to line them up in rows? That his play, which to him was a tragedy, should immediately have been perceived by audiences to be a comedy, shows that this alignment occurs without our knowing it.

Totalitarianism was devoted to the work of destroying personalities. We have attributed this depersonalization to fanaticism, which kills the individual conscience. Under totalitarianism, the subject resembles the man in the crowd described by Gustave Le Bon: he is a superficial being, that is, a being of emotions and moods. Unable to find within himself a sense of reason, which judges and questions, he is rendered permanently incapable of depth by the repetition of propaganda, which invades homes and permeates every moment of everyday life. Totalitarian man is capable of the worst crimes because, in essence, he has been robbed of his conscience. But Ionesco was intent on portraying this same loss of self in contemporary society. The reasons for this phenomenon, its development and consequences, are far removed from those associated with totalitarian depersonalization. Here there is no monstrous political party determined to make every mind fall into line. Here citizens enjoy freedom of thought and expression, which is constitutionally guaranteed and represented by the presence of multiple viewpoints in the press. However, most citizens repeat the same statements. An updated edition of the living room in *The Bald Soprano* could be created by replacing the truisms from the textbook with sentences taken from the most popular newspapers. A thought that strays from common thinking (or rather from dominant thinking, which considers itself to be commonly held) is an insult to the collectivity and is punishable by excommunication. Doesn't Copernicus's famous *sapere auso* make us long for a time that no longer exists? He dared to think for himself! Our contemporaries admire Copernicus because he struggled against the church. But they do not admire him for his independent mind. Their packaged truths have no place for any new Copernicuses.

Nonetheless, it is not the pressure of dominant opinion that directly keeps citizens from thinking beyond the bounds of conventional ideas. If this pressure can be exerted, it is only because the citizen has lost all or part of his critical consciousness. Opinion is too soft and weak to take hold of vigilant minds. It does not force itself on anyone, for it has no arguments: it flows wherever there is nothing in its way. Once any reigning assertion made its way into the living room of *The Bald Soprano,* it found an indefinitely repeated echo. What is cruelly missing in our free societies is a kind of intellectual freedom.

The absence of intellectual freedom is the greatest danger that can threaten a society. Not in the short term, since in the present, what counts most is the freedom of movement, the freedom to buy and to sell and to live as one wishes. But intellectual freedom is the only guarantee of a future. Without it, imagination dries up, and the wildest or most unrealistic theories can suddenly grip public opinion. Without intellectual freedom, obsolete habits and hackneyed prejudices spread and darken the atmosphere without challenge. Without intellectual freedom, everything gravitates toward convenience, verisimilitude, the commonplace. The most absurd ideas can become commonplaces for want of a contradictor. Without intellectual freedom, the avenue is wide open for tyrannies of all sorts.

The loss of spiritual or intellectual independence is maintained by the fear of marginalization, similar to what happened in bygone societies that had a single, dominant belief. There is nothing more terrifying for an individual than to see himself excluded from the social group. And originality of thought, today as yesterday, results in exclusion. How many people would rather remain quiet than lose social recognition? And silence, when it becomes a habit, ends up destroying thought by confining it to the closed circle of inwardness. Thus is formed a society that has nothing consensual about it except appearance, an artificial common world, its "commonality" founded on imposed views. A genuine common world would be established on expressed and accepted differences.

Where does this malleable individual come from, this being apparently so empty that he finds himself capable of unflinchingly accepting the dogmas of the most terrifying ideologies, the mindlessly repeated affirmations of soft conformity, or the new fanaticism of our democracies?

Modernity was dedicated to the liberation of man from intolerance and from the fanaticism that generates war. Fanaticism, the consequence of commonly held certitudes, is ready to reduce its adversaries by any means at its disposal. Since the seventeenth century, modernity has therefore been determined to eradicate certitudes entirely, in a slow movement that passed through Enlightenment rationalism into the philosophies of suspicion. In the course of the nineteenth century, this movement produced an individual who was ready to accept totalitarianism because he was nostalgic for lost certainties and incapable of contemplating limits, having been persuaded that everything was possible with impunity. This resulted in a character like Eichmann, who was perfectly normal yet incapable of intellectual distance. Rehearsing the views that he had been taught, he definitively made them his only "thought" until his last breath. Now, with the passing and ultimate collapse of totalitarian thinking, the spirit of the times, frightened by what it has shown itself capable of producing, finds itself unable to counter this danger. For it has not yet admitted that a vacuum of interior thought, and not certainties, gives rise to dehumanization. To this danger, it offers up the same response that it did to the old religious fanaticisms. In an even more radical way, it applies itself to the task of stripping the individual of anything that might structure his thought. The ideal then becomes to shed one's self, that is, to resist any temptation to develop personal beliefs.

We sought to crush the fanaticism of earlier certitudes by disestablishing certitudes as such. In the second half of the century, the guardians of our points of reference stopped protecting what they had in their care. What happened on a large scale was what Kafka tells of in his *Letter to Father*: the father did not transmit his religious faith to his child because he no longer knew how to justify it, and because in his own life, faith had become no more than a succession of meaningless rituals.[7] Today, not only religious rituals, but cultural knowledge, the legitimacy of institutions and politics, the taboos of child-rearing, right down to the customs of basic manners have been deemed meaningless, out of fear of the oppression they might cause. The guardians of the mind, panic-stricken at having been labeled "tyrants" by a few leading intellectuals, and little able to offer real legitimization for their habit-ridden thought, have stopped teaching. In the wasteland grows a society of individuals without depth, without their own ideas, without habits of questioning, without distance from themselves, yet who all the while assert their sublime liberty.

The rise of the modern subject comes into being through a severance from common consciousness, a breaking away from the community's protection. The subject chokes like a newborn baby who takes its first full gulp of air; he yells, and will forever retain the hazy memory of a time when differentiation did not yet exist. In difficult times he will think of it nostalgically—myths of a golden age, Dostoyevsky's parable of the Grand Inquisitor. And yet there is no returning to the past. There is only regression to the regions that look like the past but whose light has dimmed. Regression occurs when life is impoverished by one's inability or unwillingness to hold one's rank as free subject, and it remains colored by this poverty: it is always negating, refusing, rebelling. The depersonalized man of today is in mourning over the subject he cannot seem to become. It is as if the fear of leaving behind the warm womb of organic societies had not yet found a remedy; as if, in the aftermath of the various forms of dictatorship that responded to this fear, postmodern democracy were unable to respond to it either. In this sense, the Enlightenment has not come to fruition but rather stumbles blindly ahead, producing either an individual rendered lifeless through totalitarian propaganda or an empty individual, drowning in all-powerful opinion, as previously described by Tocqueville.

By defending the inalienable dignity of the individual human being, by setting the stage for the emergence of autonomous and individually responsible personal consciousness, Europe embarked on a major challenge. But Europe risks exhausting the subject by demanding too much of him. This seems indeed to be what is happening, if we look at the flight from the self that can be seen in various forms under totalitarianism, but also in the individualism of late modernity. However, the durability of the human rights ethic, which is intertwined with personal dignity, depends on the future of the subject. Henceforth, responsibility, visions of the future, and the determination of the meaning of existence will fall upon him—and no longer upon communities and collectivities. It is the subject who hopes, who can begin something. In other words, it is the subject who knows freedom, who knows that he will no longer live in anonymity. If he loses his stature and his reality, if he seeks to dissolve himself in a greater entity because he is weary or doubtful, he will drag personal dignity down with him. For if the subject does not respect himself, then on what basis can he stake a claim to respect? The subject is characterized precisely by his acceptance of self-encounter, by the pains he takes not to avoid this self-confrontation, which is bound to be tumultuous and troubling. The subject's vocation is to seek out the foundation of his own existence, to accept his responsibility in the present, and to face the idea of his own death. But he can assume his autonomy only if he is steeped in a culture, if he belongs to a world from whose structures he draws his own critical capacities. If the contemporary individual remains incapable of questioning, it is because he has been emptied of his points of reference. Having been liberated from his bearings, he has also been liberated from his judgment. But like any human faculty, judgment is not abstract; it is exercised within a cultural framework.

To escape tyranny, the remedy is not to undermine, but to build. It is humbly to propose referents, knowing them to be incomplete. The genuine subject builds without succumbing to the obsession to make things definitive. He knows he cannot build anything on sea foam. He has to lay foundations. But our ground is sand, and every truth is partial or incomplete. It takes but a single event to overturn existing lines of division, or a single new necessity to redefine priorities. The passionate desire to establish the perfect and final produces fanaticized ideologies and religions. The way out of fanaticism is not to enthrone negation but to accept contingency.

Fanaticism consists not in the subject's acceptance of exterior truths, but in his blind acceptance of the truths he defends. Because history is not finite, because we cannot fathom the depth of events, absolute certainty always escapes us. Incapable of going beyond the previous mentality, late modernity produces an ideology from every new certitude. Late modernity has not recognized the path that finite man must unsteadily travel, as if walking a tightrope. It has managed only to grasp the idea of "all or nothing," and therefore swings back and forth between nihilism and sectarianism.

We are right to reject ideologies *sensu stricto* as global conceptions of the world capable of claiming the individual in his entirety by monopolizing meaning. But we need *sensu lato* ideologies, or if one prefers, worldviews. The present defenders of economic liberalism tend to describe this system as a natural organization that is an obvious expression of simple normality. But nothing is natural in this sense, even though there are organizations that are more artificial than others, and even though some of them, through excessive artificiality, constrain humans to live in societies in which they ultimately become superfluous. The human world is always a cultural construction whose relationship to "nature" is always a matter of debate: hence the futility of the current Nietzschean rejection of "metanarratives." There is no final understanding of history, such as that conceived of in Marxism.[8] But neither is it possible for man to live without an understanding of history, happiness, and his future. In this respect, religions are worldviews; but a rejection of God is also a worldview. A contemporary philosopher who stops thinking because he is afraid of thinking falsely finds himself in the falsehood of non-thought. The demand that is put on us is not the question asking whether we want to think or not, but that we carefully protect thinking. We must give refuge to thinking, in which we wish to live and die, as to an exile in search of a homeland.

Our era remains paralyzed in a formidable either-or situation: Once the subject latches onto a truth, dedicates himself to it, and follows its ways, he sooner or later risks becoming its unconditional accomplice and henchman, destroying anything that stands in its way. But if he "frees" himself from certainty (from meaning, from truth), he locks himself into a shallow and narcissistic existence—one that paradoxically leaves him vulnerable to any new passing dogmatism.

Today, as we take every care to avoid new fanaticisms, we move from Charybdis to Scylla by rejecting out of precaution any coherent thought. It would be wiser to avoid depersonalization, the deepest source of the ills that might befall us. For the truth is not meant to be hammered into others or to be suppressed: it is to be pursued.

While late modernity produces relativism, a form of nihilism, in order to escape the fanaticism of certitudes, the postcommunist thought of Central and Eastern Europe offers an alternative, a different vision of the subject. This is apparent in the analyses the dissidents of that region have developed concerning the path out of communism. What was the philosophy that opposed communism and finally overcame it, as miraculously as David slew Goliath? It is the philosophy of rights, promulgated in the name of human dignity and democratic pluralism, but certainly not in the name of a self-made sovereign subject, unbound to any truth outside himself. For such a subject would be able to oppose communism only with his personal disapproval, his irrational indignation. That being the case, it is difficult to see how as a dissident he could defeat the communist line, since both sides would simply be locked into a subjectivity that precluded any possible argument. On the contrary, the Eastern and Central European intellectuals took up their opposition by arguing for a subject who, by consulting his conscience, is capable of invoking laws beyond those of his own subjectivity—and laws other than those promulgated by the all-powerful communist state, which is merely one nightmarish expression of modern subjectivism.

Must we then understand that these dissidents stood for a universal truth, or a purported universal truth—a religious truth, for example—in order to stand up to the communist line, which, although emanating from modern subjectivity, became nonetheless a viewpoint that purported to be objective? Some think that only a religion can fight an ideology. But we would then find ourselves in a struggle between two views of the absolute, and the modern subject would fall through the cracks. To call an imposed religion to the rescue against communism would resemble the imposture of calling communism to the rescue against fascism, as occurred in the mid-twentieth century. For the ultimate goal of the dissidents' opposition was not to have one obligatory view triumph over the other, but to restore the subject's freedom.

If he is neither self-founded (hence given over to subjectivity) nor bound to an exterior and absolute foundation (hence perhaps not a truly modern subject), who is this subject for which the dissident fights? The literature of Eastern and Central Europe, led by such figures as Jan Patocka in Bohemia and Josef Tischner in Poland, is prolific on this question. Here we see a subject unfulfilled, in contrast to the satisfied subject bequeathed by modern individualism.

Subjectivism, which produced both twentieth-century totalitarianism and contemporary individualism, issues from a subject who is self-sufficient. Lacking nothing, he draws from himself everything he needs in terms of meaning and purpose. Sovereignty is autarky, or self-sufficiency. In his self-founded sovereignty, the subject attaches value to what he draws from within himself. But he then finds himself prone to indulge in all the excesses of solipsism. It is precisely this self-sufficiency that the dissident contests, this conviction that the alpha and the omega are within oneself, this pretension of rivaling the absolute. Thus, he does not seek a subject identified with an absolute other than communism—the absolute of a religion, of yet another ideology, or simply of his own subjectivity. He seeks a subject who is enlightened by a meaning outside himself while keeping a distance from that meaning. Fully aware that foundational truths exist beyond himself (otherwise, he would be another partisan of self-sufficiency), he nevertheless refuses to identify with any truth to the point of subjugating his conscience to it. Every truth seems to him to be indefinitely problematic, and his certitudes are always a matter of debate.

While the struggle against Nazi totalitarianism gave rise to communism as yet another genealogy of self-sufficiency, the dissident subject that was forged by the fight against communism is an anxious subject. He knows that meaning and value do not spring from within like reflections of his desire. On the contrary, he knows that meanings are to be found outside himself. And yet the distance he maintains from them does not imply that he is forever in suspension, "on a search." No, he must make choices and commitments, and he knows that he will be responsible for the exterior meaning he has chosen and recognized. In other words, he will have to accept incompleteness, for as a finite subject he does not have the greatness necessary to determine meaning in its fullness. His awareness of the disproportion between his own finitude and the greatness of meaning—an awareness that implicates society and the world along with it—keeps him from identifying himself with his certitudes, which is precisely what the fanatic does. At the same time, it leaves him in dread. The discovery of a meaning will not guarantee him any rest. For no truth will ever be given to him in its entirety.

If we are willing to learn from the experience of the disaster-stricken societies of Eastern Europe, we will give birth to a subject very different from the one who inhabits our old liberal democracies today. This new subject will be aware of the necessity of meaning. But he will handle certitudes with all the precaution of an explosives expert. He will not let himself be swindled. He will no longer be endowed with meaning, but will recognize in himself a gift for meaning. He will not flinch from questions with no answers and will go through life carrying this heavy burden. He will be less at peace and less certain than in times of fanaticism, but less suicidally pretentious and also less secretly anguished than in times of nihilism. He will have added another dimension to his humanity—that of accepted uncertainty, to replace both naïve certainties and the rejection of all certainty. He will have none of the sarcasm of "Better nothing, than something incomplete!" He will no longer aspire to be the master of the world but rather to be a clear-minded actor in a world recognized as unfinished.

It is now up to us to allow the subject to strengthen and structure himself in order to act as a bulwark against future tyrannies. It is not truth that oppresses. It is the subject himself who opens the way to oppression, in two inextricably related ways. Either he claims to be self-sufficient in his apprehension of truth, and henceforth identifies himself with it, making himself at home in the *fanum*, the sanctuary where fanaticism is born; or else, stripped naked by being deprived of his points of reference, he becomes easy prey to the dominant discourse, which engulfs and consumes all his faculties. Here the subject lives unawares in a *fanum*, which he does not even recognize as such. Messages from authority, religions (whether revealed or not), and ideologies have no authority in themselves: it is in men's minds that reverence does or does not reside. The current fear of universal truths reflects our self-distrust. It is an admission of weakness.

We tire ourselves in a futile search for harmless certitudes, or in draining the sea of referents in order to eliminate the monsters that dwell therein. But the self-founded subject is every bit as capable of terrorism as is the subject who bears witness to an exterior truth. His emotions and moods also take on the character of the absolute. It is not the absence of truth that liberates the subject, but the distance between him and truth. The essential question is whether the subject maintains a sufficient margin of detachment from his certitudes so as not to become their slave. The construction of a common world, as opposed to the antiworld of totalitarianism and the nonworld of contemporary relativism, will depend entirely on the ability of the subject to accept incomplete certitudes. If the coming era is to move beyond both ideological oppression and nihilism, it will be able to do so only by accepting the disquietude of the thinking subject.

The philosophy of rights can thus accommodate two distinct subjects: the self-founded subject, refusing any external and overarching truth, and the uneasy subject who maintains a certain distance from those truths that do arise. In the uneasy subject, concern for the truth replaces concern for oneself, or rather, the former involves the latter. He is characterized by an awareness that he is not, in and of himself, the absolute—in other words, by a certain humility. The self-founded subject, on the other hand, is both self-sufficient and self-important—both complete and pretentious. These terms speak volumes: by saying he is self-sufficient, he makes the *pretense* of being self-sufficient, for no human being could really be so. Our completeness, as soon as it is uttered, becomes vanity, presumptuousness, boasting. But it is properly human to seek truth without ever attaining it in its perfect form. Indeed, man is never more human than when he is embarked on this feverish quest. What Jan Patocka called "living in truth" is not the mind's complete embrace of an external message, but life lived in recognition of the problem posed by the hoped-for but elusive truth. Man's truth lies in the unceasing quest for truths outside himself. The twentieth century has bequeathed to us a disaster-stricken subject: to save the subject would mean to save the search for truth.

The uneasy subject is spared the fatal choice between fanaticism and nihilism. He is not the contemporary "open-minded man," who accepts every passing thing and refuses to judge in order to avoid the accusation of intolerance. The uneasy subject has no reason to accept just any assertion at all, for he knows the pretension of bearers of absolutes, under whatever name their absolute might go by. Yet he believes in the existence of truth, and he seeks it. On the other hand, he never totally possesses a truth, for he knows himself to be definitively incomplete, incapable of ever encompassing what can be known of being and existence. Before all other certainties, he is certain of his own finiteness, of his powerlessness to reveal the whole of being, of his incapacity completely to comprehend.

It is very possible, in this sense, that faith in transcendence might just be the best bulwark against fanaticism, because it ensures the subject's sense of his own finiteness. Jean-Pierre Vernant writes in *Entre mythe et politique,* "For those of us who belonged to the Marxist tradition and in some ways still do, and who think that any reference to an objectified transcendence conceived in the form of a doctrine inevitably generates risks of totalitarianism because the reference then becomes an instrument for transforming society in the name of this doctrine, it is not always comfortable to hear, for example, certain Czech intellectuals explain that objectified transcendence is no longer, once it is stated in finite and therefore human terms, that transcendence is itself not object but rather movement, not substance but the surpassing of the finite, and that a transcendence so conceived is, in their eyes, the only guarantee of freedom for the individual, to the extent that, rooted in a non-objectified notion, it at the same time allows the individual to find within himself what he needs to question every limitation, and every oppression he may experience. Seen from this angle, whatever intellectual uneasiness this analysis might cause us, the religious dimension has indeed played (and will perhaps continue to play) an undeniable role, that of offering the best guarantee of liberty and the best foundation upon which to resist totalitarianism."[9] Religion can, of course, give rise to sectarianism. But at the same time it represents the best bulwark against sectarianism. We will have to set aside the simplistic thinking according to which it is sufficient simply to eliminate anything that threatens to do harm. What threatens is also what saves.

This difficult relationship with certainty, characteristic of contemporary Western societies, can be seen in the subject's inauthenticity. Whether he possesses a so-called certain truth or rejects all truths, the subject seems aloof and dishonest. The subject becomes authentic when he concerns himself with the truth. He uncovers the truth about himself only through an uneasy awareness that the truth is always only partly unveiled. There is a contradiction here that is particular to the nature of man's being, because he can have nothing more than a painful, questioned certainty, an uncertain certainty. This is why indifference toward truth, like aggressively asserted truth, always exposes a liar in flight from himself. And it is very much this escapist subject in flight from himself that we see today. The subject will stop fleeing only when he accepts the risk of ever-problematic commitments.

The modern subject can be identified by this search for meaning: if he runs away from this task, he stops being a subject and loses the only mode of existence open to him. When that happens, it is often because he fears giving himself an illusory or even dangerous meaning. He will argue that the young Nazi and the young Komsomol freely gave a meaning to their lives—would it not have been better for them to have remained in meaninglessness? The answer is no. It would have been better for them to have found a different meaning. The attribution of meaning implies a certain risk. But if man is unwilling to take this risk, he will never become a subject. If he must shy away from this adventure, we will eventually long for a return to holistic societies, ones in which meaning was handed down as part of one's heritage. For by remaining in non-meaning, man becomes a mere spectator of his own existence, which is in fact no longer an existence: nothing can happen to him anymore, no event takes on meaning, events and circumstances slide past him without his being able to give them a name. Nothing in his life seems either fortunate or unfortunate, because he does not want to make a *determination*, and from that point on, he himself is nothing. All he has left is to play a role on the stage of appearances, that is, to usurp the determinations imposed upon him from without and pretend that they are his own, always tentatively and without engaging them. The tentative and the spectacular are cut from the same cloth.

The guarantee against fanaticism is not to be found in the subject's detachment, but in the subject's conviction that he is finite and insufficient. It is identification with a point of reference that leads to fanaticism, not identification with what is at stake. The authentic subject is constructed with the latter. The subject risks himself for justice or liberty—absent which the moral act remains devoid of authenticity. But he is not himself justice or liberty; he cannot speak in their name or take their measure. He does not doubt the truth of his chosen referent—otherwise, would he put himself on the line to fight for it? But he is always doubting how well his act measures up to his ideal. He wonders whether this is the best way to serve the ideal to which he has committed himself. He wonders whether he has been able to define the point of reference accurately. This lack of certainty reflects the risk undertaken by the subject in his finiteness. He knows he is neither justice nor liberty, but rather a servant, inadequate and unguided, of their realization, which is never fully known. He errs on the side of making adjustments, because he is always inadequate for the causes he defends. His judgments and acts are inspired by the referent, which he can never quite grasp in its entirety. He belongs to the truth. The truth does not belong to him, but exudes from every part of him.

The subject who knows that he is operating in uncertainty as he fine-tunes his points of reference remains open to his times. A new event can penetrate his inner world, forcing him to patch up or rework his self-evident truths. Otherwise stated: something can actually happen to him because he knows he is not exempt from contradiction, from preconceived notions accepted without proof, from false semblances, contrivance, and superficiality. He accepts that reality will disrupt his certitudes, forcing him to readjust his acts and his points of reference. He understands that events will disrupt the order of the world, open up hidden meanings, and break through the surface, revealing the permanence of the essential questions that lie beneath like a storm raging beneath the calm surface of the sea. What happens in the world can take on meaning for him, for he is full of being. He is nourished by signs that illuminate, that focus in on and secure or reject outside forces. He possesses within himself the necessary structures to understand and judge what comes upon him.

Fanaticism arises when the subject forgets this unequal relationship and his intrinsic finiteness, taking himself for the point of reference, equating himself with it, believing himself to be its sole interpreter or even its source. We see today how the partisans of human rights can themselves become fanatics, casting their adversaries into the shadows and speaking *ex cathedra* as if they were the reference points personified. This new phenomenon illustrates well that sectarianism is not only attached to certain dogmatic or totalitarian ideologies, but rather stems from the way in which the subject situates himself with respect to his points of reference.

Our contemporary, having rejected dangerous doctrines, now believes himself delivered from the temptation of intolerance. But the *fanum* is potentially present in each one of us, like the temptation to mistake the concrete manifestation of values for values themselves. It is the ignorance of human finiteness that animates and consolidates the *fanum*. This ignorance has turned the subject into the disaster victim of late modernity.

The genuine subject is the one who, in his quest for an ever-elusive truth, inscribes his very existence on the pathway of this indecisive quest. The authentic subject is neither a fanatic nor a nihilist, but a witness.

CHAPTER 9
THE FIGURE OF THE WITNESS

Probably because of the influence of Kantianism,[1] we live today under the reign of the morality of intention. The way in which the question of communism has been treated and the manner in which its consequences have been swept under the rug clearly reveal our state of mind in this regard. It is now acceptable to think that the consequences of seventy years of communism have only a very relative importance and that this period should not raise too much indignation in view of the purity of its goals and nobility of its discourse. This is probably why, after 1989 and as soon as the borders of the Eastern bloc were opened and tongues were free to speak, very few journalists, writers, or sociologists seemed to care much about the enormous mass of crimes that had taken place behind the "curtain." No one took an interest in enumerating these disasters, with the exception of the editors of *The Black Book of Communism,*[2] who were immediately vilified and ostracized by their colleagues and dominant opinion.[3] The infamous prison in Pitesti, where brothers and friends were forced to torture each other, the unspeakable abuses in Stasi-run prisons, the nuclear experiments to which whole populations in the Soviet Union's southern republics were subjected: all this aroused the indignation of only a few people on the fringes. Have we become cynical? Surely not, since we vigorously condemn the crimes of the Nazis. But the key to understanding the different way in which Nazi crimes and communist atrocities are treated is to be found in the morality of intention: he whose intention is considered pure is absolved in advance and forever after, regardless of the real crimes he sponsored or covered up in complicit silence.

The attitude of intentional blindness in the face of experience, the refusal to "learn the lesson" of events, is indicative of an effort, peculiar to our time, to rescue intentions. It essentially involves the history of Marxism and its numerous forms and expresses the indelible fascination that this current of thought has exerted on Western minds. More profoundly, this attitude is linked to the demiurgic ambition generated by the Enlightenment, which Marxism adopted as its own and built upon, attempting to carry it to its apex. Since the facts have incontestably shown that communism cannot be achieved in reality, every effort is made to safeguard the original intentions. Yet for this to occur, those intentions must be immunized against any contact with reality, protected from any comparison with actual experience. Acts tend to go off track and deviate; only the *intention* of Goodness can be perfect, and yet what is a will deprived of its act? Unpleasant encounters with the facts are avoided by taking refuge in the intention, which moves about in the world of ideas, cloaked in a clear conscience. The revolt against the market economy and capitalism indicates a refusal to see a definitively vicious intention—profit-seeking—spur a virtuous process—economic development.[4] The Intention is so essential that it neutralizes its effects: communism is excusable in spite of its crimes; capitalism is unacceptable in spite of its positive results.

This attitude stifles societal projects. Intention is not endeavor, but an idea without desire, an indecisive idea. A society that sustains itself on unrealized and unrealizable objectives moves into the future with reluctance.

The morality of intention resides in the realm of both purist idealism and appearance. It is totally pure because it can claim an unswerving sense of noble purpose, as described by Max Weber. There is no risk of being polluted or blurred by reality. The morality of intention never goes beyond appearance—that is, gesticulated thought—because it does not materialize in concrete form. These two characteristics make it the only morality accessible to an era that finds reality repugnant and wants nothing but perfection. Since nothing in existence is perfect, only my intention and the expression of it can be perfect. Contemporary morality is therefore nothing other than pharisaism, for it is concerned not with acting morally, but of stating the good in the form of admonishment, advice, or threats. The ad nauseum repetitiveness of moral discourse aims to give a deceiving concreteness to intention, so ethereal, and when devoid of action, so vain. Any talk of forgiveness, for example, is for others: we demand repentance, but we never forgive.

In the moralism of intention, the subject remains inauthentic, since he is reduced to ways of being in which his being is not engaged. When intention eclipses action, the individual cannot say he is acting morally, because he has not invested anything more than his appearance and his words. But on their own, these are worthless. He invests only just what it takes to *seem* moral in his own eyes and in the eyes of others. There may be within him a disguised cynicism, but generally he is nothing more than an impostor. The moralist seems to be moral, and he may even be admired. We see him photographed amid the ruins of war, holding a Bosnian child whom he has saved from the latest fascist regime. The posture is moral: it points to the Good. But any moral posture smacks precisely of imposture, and he who calls in the cameras to show the good he proposes to do is very likely interested more in his own glory than in the act itself. Moral action, when inspired by personal conscience, reveals the falseness of publicity. A moral code entirely given over to publicity is really no morality at all, even if it has all the trappings of one. Hence the contradiction of an era devoted to appearance, yet passionate about ethics, a contradiction that can be understood by positing that ours is an ethics of intention.

When authenticity is no longer a requirement, cynicism may result. Yet pharisaism results more often because morals remain deeply human, undoubtedly rooted in nature, and those who do not apply them will at least want to look as if they do. One simply does not seem human when one rejects morals. The less one applies them, the more ostentatious the appearance of morality must be.

This speciousness generally develops among old-country elites, who, replete with knowledge and experience, bored and weary, do not really know where the Good is to be found—if it exists at all. They therefore cling to their own egos as the only sure authority when all else has disappeared. And yet personal reputations cannot be made without taking moral positions. The challenge then is to speak out powerfully in favor of morality without sacrificing the better part of one's existence to it.

Human beings have a sense of belonging to a world when they share what is essential, and what is essential is determined by actions. The contemporary subject talks much and acts little, or rather, acts without risking himself, preferably in front of cameras. He is intelligent and cowardly, a not unusual combination in self-satisfied times: sophistication, over centuries, develops the mind but disarms the will. The transformation of many humanitarian activities into spectacles reveals the nonworld in its wake. A republic of beautiful minds is not a world: to think and to talk is not to live, just as intentions repeatedly asserted do not constitute morality.

The present state of affairs most likely reflects our decrepitude, our weariness with morality, and not just the adaptation of morality to the spirit of the times. The nobility of conscience that is characteristic of the genuine moral subject is an ephemeral figure in history, as fragile as it is demanding. In fact, self-truth is not so much a state of being as a voyage into a storm. Entire eras grow weary of the struggle. Bartolomé de Las Casas described in this way the Christian missionaries of the early centuries: "Their life was in perfect accord with what they were teaching."[5] He thought that the abandonment of this consistency explained Christianity's deviation from its path in the sixteenth century. Where could the revolt of Hus or Luther have come from, if not from the gaps that widened over the centuries between what the clerics said and how they lived?

Today, as in the sixteenth century, dominant thought believes it no longer needs to bear witness. Hence the feeling of imposture: Sartre admitted saying one thing to the average working person and something else to his peers, but today we live in a society in which everything smacks of falsehood—from deliberate lies about Pol Pot to the pharisaism of some humanitarian undertakings.

A common world is woven together from the roots: from the unanswerable questions that weigh painfully on each individual, to which each can respond only through acts in which existence itself is at stake. Only action engages being and shapes the subject. And it is the convergence of paths that binds people together. During the war in Kosovo, the only thing members of Western societies shared was the trading of insults and accusations of evil intentions: the distant bombings of civilians-cum-monsters was not an act worthy of the stakes involved, since it engaged only technology; these bombings were an intention disguised as a moral act, the simulated act of the society of the spectacular. Our societies are not composed of authentic subjects, capable of putting themselves on the line to back up what they say. We state what is morally correct and believe we have created a social bond. Yet each individual sets up a distinct separation between his personal existence, given over to his own subjectivity, and common opinion, to which he adds his voice from a distance, without risking even a hair of his own.

Communion between human beings grows out of the struggles they share in facing the mysteries of life. The personal bonds forged in war are well known. Yet it is hardly necessary to invent wars in order to build a community. Life's questions fuel just as many struggles; in them is revealed the subject who is willing to stand at the heart of this questioning, where he meets other subjects. The inevitably endless debate over essential issues should structure the common world of modern human beings, who have taken upon themselves the responsibility for determining meaning. If the subject is no longer a bearer of revealed truths, he may still bear witness to his questioning about truth through acts that signify. A modern common world is not made up of *disciples*, but of *witnesses*, because the modern subject knows that the truth remains incomplete and that his grasp of the good remains partial and always too fragile. If he wants to show that he believes in the existence of the good, his only recourse is to become a witness to this incompleteness.

In the 1999 Balkan conflict, an authentic subject would have been able either to risk his life for the victims of Milosevic or to refrain from giving morality lectures to all the world's barbarians. Morality lessons are taught only to children, in order to show them how to behave, or else are imparted by practicing what one teaches—at least, if one hopes to lay claim to being truthful and effective. These exceptions aside, morality concerns only the individual conscience: "Morally man can condemn only himself, not another—or, if another, then only in the solidarity of charitable struggles. No one can morally judge another. It is only where the other seems to me like myself that the closeness reigns which in free communication can make a common cause of what finally each does in solitude."[6] And morality is valid only through action: only its concrete manifestation establishes, justifies, and disseminates it. Morality is not a science or knowledge that can stand on thought alone; morality is a practice. This explains why the heart of the inauthentic moralist beats only for distant and unattainable causes (in space and time): this gives him an excuse for not taking moral action and for remaining all talk. It is very difficult to preach morality to one's neighbor without applying it to oneself: by his very presence, the other bears witness to the imposture and casts reproach in the face of the pharisee. When the other is far removed, however, there is no reproachful look. The pharisee therefore has every interest in reserving his moral discourse for the distant other, while he writes his neighbor off as a loss, on the argument that he is free to do what he wishes.

There may be a historical constant here, one in which concern shifts from the close-to-home to the far away as the courage to become involved weakens and the subject's authenticity along with it. In first-century B.C. Rome, the crumbling of the *res publica* as a close-by common world favored the spread of the idea of the oneness of humankind, an ethic for a vast world composed of far-away men, to whom it would undoubtedly be far less costly to show respect.[7] A dramatic compensation followed: the disintegration of bonds with one's neighbor caused the essential need for communion to shift to a less demanding elsewhere. However, the distant world cannot replace the nearby world. The distant completes and extends the near, but the wellspring that makes this possible is personal risk undertaken in the moral deed, and when that wellspring runs dry, the whole edifice is destroyed. This is why a restoration of the subject will require first an understanding that one's neighbor is the initial other in moral life.

When morality plays out on a stage that is external to the subject, the result is a world of appearance and pharisaism: here morality is only something one talks about, as one talks about an event happening on the other side of the world. What is at stake is one's reputation or image in the eyes of others, or oneself considered as an actor on the stage, where one must play one's part in order to gain recognition. Moral statements become the rules of the game, which are simultaneously both at stake and required for victory. Procedure—the words to be used and the way to use them—is all that counts. Stoicism has made a strong comeback in contemporary thought because it proposes a vision of existence as a role to be played with detachment. It rejects the feeling that life is tragic, demands spectator status for the self, and refuses to engage life's mysteries, all in order to avoid suffering. It considers action vulgar, as agitation that can only result in torment. The stoic is not a subject, but a detached gaze, holding in disdain both the tragic questions and that action which alone can respond to them.

The setting in which the moralist postures is one where acts are both collective and sheep-like. By brandishing the Good, the moralist drowns in insignificance, like the comic character whose lines are so frivolous that from time to time he physically disappears from the view of the other characters. Ethical values have this unique characteristic: they have a highly symbolic value in discourse, but take on meaning only when they compel the subject. Although an act carried out under constraint could never be a moral act, a human being becomes a true subject only when he feels compelled by and bears witness to the values he himself has chosen. He brings them into concrete reality only by putting himself on the line as their guarantor.

The society of the spectacular naturally accompanies individualism: Narcissus prefers to play at life rather than actually to live it, because he loves himself, not the meaning with which he would have to identify were he actually to live life. The society of the spectacular naturally accompanies moment-to-moment existence: the glory of appearance is ephemeral but easily attained, since it is sufficient just to appear. To actually *be* is so arduous and uncertain. When the society of appearance survives long enough, it eventually leads to spectacles of spectacle in the theaters, either out of derision, as in Ionesco's plays, or literally, as in the plays of Sartre, which create an overwhelming sense of falseness. The society of the spectacular lives in a monumental imposture and forgets what the truth of existence might be. In the end, only the encounter with death can remind the subject that he exists as such. On the day of this encounter, he will have to unequivocally put his existence on the table as the real stake in the game. Death does not put up with shams and boasts: after a whole life spent on the stage of an imaginary theatre, in his final hour Nero took off his mask. Let us wager—without being excessively optimistic, however—that moralism's deception will destroy itself. The imminent downfall of a sermonizer who does not act on his own words is assured: all it takes is one citizen to cry out that the emperor has no clothes.

As always, minority groups more often bear witness to their convictions, precisely because they are in the minority. Having long since lost power and the public's ear, they have only their actions left to speak for them. If one were to bet on the future, one might predict with a good chance of success that currents of thought that are devoid of witnesses thereby sign their own death warrants and have not much time to live. Wherever there are subjects who take action in their personal lives and are not just full of talk, there is sure to be a future.

The witness is he for whom life and thought are inseparable. He lives his words just as he breathes. This is why he gives little advice and never preaches. For he knows the importance of words, which for him are not something one wears around one's neck to enhance one's appearance but rather carry weight. Jan Patocka calls this "life in the truth." He died during a police interrogation, after having become head of Charter 77, the resistance movement that sprouted under the Czech communist government.

There is no false moralism in the witness because, while it is difficult to live virtuously, it is impossible to achieve complete morality in daily existence; only a god, no mere hero, could do such a thing. That is why moralistic discourse, omnipresent in today's society, is the palpable and tangible sign of imposture. It serves as an excuse for not living in virtue, which must be practiced before it is preached.

The authentic subject leaves a mark on the world through his words-become-deeds. His actions, like the strides of someone walking in wet sand, are weighty and deep. The subject carves his presence deep into reality.

The authentic subject puts himself at stake on the gaming table. He identifies with what is at stake in the ethical act. For him, the ethical life is no theatrical stage, behind which real life is happening, but life itself, with its ups and downs, all of which are enveloped in the smell of death. The authentic subject puts himself on the line, and this is why he cannot escape from coherence: ethical deeds carried out in an aimless, haphazard way would shatter him. This is also why he has no interest in publicity: the gravity of the act goes far beyond the grandiloquence of any discourse. Ultimately it is he himself who is in question, exposed to every wind. If the adventure some-how goes awry, it will be he who is torn asunder and put to flight.

The purpose of ethical action is to give concrete expression to val-ues that without it would remain mere talk. No value has concrete expression except through a subject who answers for it, who stakes himself for it, and who bears witness to it. Justice exists only if there are just beings. The authentic subject offers himself as living proof that values are not merely words; he brings his weight to bear on the world in order to change it, risks his being in his moral decision-making. If he thereby walks a tightrope and pays heavy tribute to the truth as much as to the values he defends, it is because he finds here, as nowhere else, self-achievement. The moral act is a test because of the risks it entails, but only through this *test* can the subject *prove* what he is. The subject puts himself on the line so that he can demon-strate that he really is what he is not yet known to be. Often, he does not yet know it of himself: will I be able to really do what I say? Engagement in moral action is a movement from the virtual to the real, from words to reality, from appearance to truth. The moral act delivers the phantom self into reality, gives substance to the dream of hope, and transforms the imaginary subject into an authentic subject.

But here we see some of the most flagrant anthropological errors of the ideologies in whose shadow we still live: the modern subject will not find his happiness merely by being provided the products and institutions that might bring him the good he desires. Because he is endowed with the freedom to take action on his own behalf, the subject finds his happiness—the purpose of ethics—in a trial in which he seeks harmony within the self and between the self and the world. The man of holistic societies is not a full-fledged subject, in that his moral acts do not result from a genuine personal and free choice. His happiness results less from personal trial than from his ability to integrate a previously defined world order without rebel-ling. But the individual of modern welfarist societies is not a full-fledged subject either, to the extent that he has been taught that happiness will come from a source other than himself—in general, from a variety of rights—and is not achieved through his own acts. He considers happiness to be something that is owed to him.

Unemployment in contemporary welfare state is a form of *unhappiness* for the individual, but a *trial* for the state. The state bears the burden of proof, because it must prove that it is fulfilling its role. It is held responsible for the failure or inadequacy of the policies it adopts. The individual either passively accepts—considering this misfortune his fate—or rebels—considering this misfortune an injustice. Passive acceptance and revolt keep the subject from self-realization by maintaining in him the eternal temptation to hold someone or something other than himself responsible. Injustices do of course exist, and justice is served by calling them by their name. But to hold them solely responsible for individual misfortune is to hold the subject in contempt, to diminish him by depriving him of his fight against adversity, in which the combatant takes the measure of himself and finds his identity. He who has never had the occasion to take the measure of himself will never fully become himself. The error of welfarism is to believe that man can begin to develop his potentialities only when he is provided with the means. This is only partially true. In the refugee camps of Southeast Asia, observers have noticed that the boat people, having come out of terrible trials with the courage of steel, stopped making any effort at all to make their own way after receiving full assistance for a while. Man is made in such a way that too much difficulty crushes him—hence the need for solidarity; but too much protection deprives him of his own development.

Refusal to recognize the importance of trial in the creation of the subject—trial in the sense of a difficulty to be overcome, not vexation—seems to come from two intersecting postulates. First, too little value is placed on individual autonomy relative to material values as concerns well-being. Second, the greatest social equality possible is sought. The welfarist society considers worthless the growth of the self that comes from acquiring something through one's own effort; it operates on the principle that the value of the good received is all that counts. Through this reasoning, the welfarist society gives priority to equality. Whereas the possibility of acquiring goods autonomously leads to social stratification based on ability, under its system, everyone demands an equal share. But this is certainly not how to foster the emergence of genuine subjects. In the welfarist view, the individual is not considered responsible for what happens to him, as if all life's events were governed by the "destiny" of the ancient Greeks, or as if "society," an abstract entity that seems to have its strings pulled by some god, must answer completely for the problems of unemployment, discrimination, illness, divorce, and poor child-rearing.

With a view to restoring the subject, a number of voices are now questioning the welfare state's systems of assistance. Amartya Sen, Nobel Prize winner for economics in 1998, develops in this sense the concept of *capability*. Bringing out the ability of each individual to achieve autonomy within his circumstances, he calls for goods to be provided externally only when they are needed to compensate for recognized inabilities.[8] Sen suggests that each individual be given the opportunity to prove himself according to his capabilities: he calls for a solidarity that does not inhibit the development of authentic subjects. The individual who lives in a climate where desire gives rise to revolt, not to demands upon the self, is unable to know who he is. But in order to make the emergence of the subject possible, egalitarian ambitions will have to be set aside: the trial of the self results in distinctions.

Trial both makes the subject and distinguishes him. The adventure of the trial of the self is personal and cannot be reduced to a generalized experience: the subject identifies himself through this adventure, which he experiences with a sense of his uniqueness. The individuals of the welfarist society all receive the same lot in terms of what is their due and sometimes even in terms of what they should think. Such individuals find it difficult to know who they are as individuals. The modern subject is distinguished by what comes from the self: his act confers a name upon him. To exist as such, he has to be able to *begin* something, and this is undoubtedly where his real greatness lies: man in holistic societies, far from being a hero, did little more than *maintain* something. The importance of beginnings to a life's destiny cannot be overemphasized. At stake in the trial is the very identity of the subject, which is not, or is no longer, given in the cradle. This development cannot be seen as anything but human enrichment. Yet the conditions for this enrichment must still be accepted in terms of risk. I am given my identity neither by nature nor by birth, and if it is in part forged through my undertakings and actions, how could I shrink from this risk? And if I do circumvent it, and if nature and birth no longer suffice to define who I am, then who am I?

As the subject approaches existence, he is mere promise, a vague promise in which what he hopes for is part of his being; he makes himself through his actions. This is why the emergence of the subject is understood as requiring time, as an unfolding of possibilities. At every step, one runs the risk of catastrophic possibilities. In terms of hope, the future is *other*, an adventure in the sense of *ad-venir*—what is to come. The self-sufficient man lives in a prolonged instant, because he lacks an imagined future. He lives in repetition, and goes from the same to the same, like a prisoner serving a life sentence. The perpetual present is a cell, too narrow to contain reparations and forgiveness, and consequently too narrow to contain failure. At times, the perpetual present plunges the individual into boredom, if his gaze is not cast beyond the horizon of the self.[9] Boredom in this sense closely resembles the boredom experienced by the non-subjects of previous societies, who were so strongly bound to the given order that they could not engage in any new beginnings of their own. The characteristic boredom of the idle woman of the old bourgeois classes resembles that of the postmodern individual: today, the future is unimagined; then, the future was too predetermined to be imagined as something to be crafted. But it also happens that the perpetual present plunges the individual into perpetual disappointment if his gaze dares to look with envy on other destinies. Consider the anguished inhabitant of Huxley's *Brave New World*: the present never satisfies him, for his fears find neither consolation nor response in the branches of time, past or future. It is very much in an attempt to fight these two avatars of anguish—boredom and disappointment—that he is given a drug to be taken in daily doses: the effect of Huxley's soma pill is to sacralize the present. The uneasiness of the authentic subject is also very real, but it is meaningful: in this case, lack becomes hope, because time remains open-ended. His uneasy feeling carries a promise.

An existence lived out only in the present can, in exceptional circumstances, ensure that the subject is rooted in his history—on the condition that this present is directly linked to the dimension of eternity. For Jews, the present may take primacy over time because eternity is always potentially contained, or awaited, in the present.[10] The same possibility exists for the Christian: monastic time is concentrated in an instant that is directly accountable to eternity. Here the subject lives out his present under the eye of another presence, before which his whole being stands without a backward look or a future ambition. Like the traveler ready to leave in the middle of the night, he keeps his suitcase with all his possessions close to his bed while he sleeps. Here, the present moment is detached from the past and the future; it escapes through the top into eternity. This present, filled with a hope irreducible to time, obviously has nothing to do with the empty present of our modern, self-sufficient man.

If it is characteristic of the human being to be aware of his own finiteness, he may, like the Chinese sage or the stoic whom this age finds so fascinating, view this finiteness as blind fate, turning insufficiency into sufficiency. The authentic subject, on the other hand, accepts the discomfort of his paradoxes. He knows himself to be structured because his being is incomplete. He remains anxious. All that he has been given is élan. The rest is up to him. A part of him lives in hope. His hope enables him to grow, but in semi-darkness, rather than in the sunny despair that is now preferred. Furthermore, in contrast to the contemporary individual, the authentic subject knows himself to be not self-founded, but founded on a debt: the culture that has preceded him promises and permits him the status of subject. He has the capacity for autonomy, but he must win his autonomy by slowly learning to take responsibility for his own choices. He is not born a subject. But he may become one, and this is his primary hope. The self-founded individual has nothing to look forward to: he believes he already possesses everything.

The self-sufficient individual resembles the individual that Dostoyevsky's Grand Inquisitor might have created: complete, he is thus liberated from his freedom and from the anxiety of achieving his own completeness. The authentic subject has an intimate sense that he is incomplete, only half-created. Marie Balmary writes that the creator in Genesis stayed his hand before completing his work, leaving it unfinished: the only way to confer freedom.[11] The authentic subject does not see himself as a passive being built entirely by the order of a world that determines him (as in Eastern wisdom traditions or in the deformed Christianity of the Grand Inquisitor). Nor does he regard himself as solely the work of the self (as in contemporary existentialism), but rather as a gift that he himself must complete, in which "humans are not only the portrait, but also the painter, that is, are not themselves without their own involvement."[12]

The authentic subject lives on the uncertain ground between an insufficient reality and what he senses to be a fuller one, attainable only in small pieces. The purpose of action is to bridge this distance, but its mode is always tragic, because the expanse is unbridgeable. Self-sufficient man acts solely out of self-preservation, seeking to replicate the circumstances that make him self-sufficient. In this respect, his action resembles that of the primitive, who is thrown into a hostile world and forced to muster all his efforts just to survive. One might believe that the way of hope is an advancement for humanity, an emergence from primitive stagnation. But this advancement is unavoidably accompanied by anguish and worry, for the process is precarious, undertaken sometimes in vain, and full of risk. Moral action comes at the cost of this risk. If this risk is not accepted, there will only be moral theatrics, a sham ethics undertaken by masked actors, and not by beings of flesh and blood.

CHAPTER 10
COMMON VALUES AS LANGUAGE

European relativism has arisen out of a fear of intolerance. Late modernity regards any proselyte as the prophet of a new moralism, any church as a potential sect, any belief as potentially sparking a fundamentalist movement. Universalist claims are hunted down in the name of tolerance. It is supposed that an individual without beliefs will let others exist as they wish, since he has nothing to impose upon them.

Cultural relativism, however, does not spell the end of the history of fanaticism. On the contrary, it gives rise to the fanaticism of particularity.

The history of violence reveals that war and oppression seek their justifications not as a means of disseminating allegedly universal ideas, but as a means of spreading a certain way of life. One people oppresses another in the name of its supposed greatness, of its importance considered from its own point of view. Virtually every war in history has had the conquest of territory as its goal, which, with few exceptions, constitutes the foundation and the primary condition for a people's existence. Historically, oppression has been perpetrated in the name of what could be called *truths of being*.

It is in Europe that we first see wars fought in the name of *conceptual truths*—doctrines, ideologies, religions, or other universal claims: conquests become missions. This has been true practically from the outset, from the democracy of Pericles through Christianity to communism and regimes dedicated to human rights; it always has been "good news" that has legitimized conquest, war, and constraints of all sorts. This progressed to the point that Europe came to identify herself with the concept of the universal, only the content of which changed over the ages. In this respect Europe has been unique.

Thus, the relativism of late modernity does not presage a future characterized by tolerance, but rather a change in the justification of conflict. With the disappearance of certainties, struggle and oppression in Europe will no longer take place in the name of conceptual truths but in the name of truths of being. The end of universal claims does not herald a peace of joyous indifference, but the end of the European vision of the oneness of the human species, a vision that undergirded its age-old universalism. The new relativism opens the way toward pre-European or extra-European modes of thought.

At the international level, the ebbing of conceptual truths has not led to peace during the past few decades. It has eliminated a certain type of war fought under the banner of universal ideas, but that abandoned ground has allowed for the development of nationalistic or ethnic conflicts. Fanaticism has found new justifications. In our Western societies, we once secularized the state in order to avoid wars of religion; these wars were replaced by those between secularized ideologies. Now relativism has opened the way for struggles between different identity groups.

Ideological oppression has the systematic nature that any doctrine can boast of having. Violent clashes between different identity groups, on the other hand, are marked by explosions of passion—less orderly but no less savage. The former may find an antidote in bad conscience, as was the case in colonialist wars, whereas the latter may sputter out from weariness. Both doctrine and self-certainty soften in time, and time also erodes justifications. But fanaticism is at work in both cases, so that we would be hard pressed to say which was worse. Every great human catastrophe is unique. No one would like to have to choose between wars over universals or wars over particulars. One certainty remains, however: the rejection of universal truths does not ensure peace. For danger resides not only in doctrines, but also in the will to power, which, if necessary, legitimizes itself. One might say that the will to power is at times an end—in the case of *truths of being*—and at times a mere means—in the case of *conceptual truths*—but is always present. The peoples who until recently sought to conquer in the name of a principle—the USSR in the name of communism and the United States in the name of liberty—will still be able to conquer in their own name, in the name of greater Russia or glorious America.

The break with the past that delegitimized European universalism in the twentieth century—guilt about colonialism and the terrorism of deadly ideologies—has not relegated certitudes to the confines of our societies: it has destroyed them entirely. The reason is obvious: European certitudes are universal because they always rest upon our quasi-congenital postulate of the unity of the human species. What interests us alone does not interest us at all. An Asian may be a Buddhist without thinking of proselytizing. But if a European is a Christian or a communist, it is for the entire world. The rejection of universalism thus leads directly to relativism: if our models do not hold for all peoples, how could they possibly hold only for ourselves?

Thus, in the heart of contemporary societies, different ways of being have begun to demand recognition, ready to defend themselves not through an appeal to ideals about how to reshape society, but based on the claims of identity. Citizens would become indignant if asked to fight for universal *models,* which no longer are compelling. They now fight for *modes* of existence. The society of late modernity is populated by an assortment of groups, each demanding its right to be recognized. These groups may be based on different biological, behavioral, ethnic, or legal identities, or else on convictions or ideals that have become rare. They therefore refrain from proselytism. Conceptual truths have not been entirely lost, but the convictions they rest on no longer mean the same thing: a group may call itself Catholic or Protestant, but it will do so not in order to spread the Good News, but rather merely to affirm its identity. In other words, *conceptual truths*, the building blocks of coherent worldviews and views of life, function as if they were *truths of being*, for they now serve only to reinforce individuals and groups in their particularity. When a statement of universal truth does survive, it is in the service of the individual who needs it as a label. But the individual no longer assumes the role of that truth's messenger; he is no longer in its service. In the very understanding of the "meaning of existence," there has been a reversal of ends. It is as if the sovereign individual, realizing that he would be empty, hollow, and lacking in identity if he did not connect to some reference outside of himself, stuck a label on his forehead in order to carry a name. But he does not really adhere to its underlying truth to the point of actually wanting to persuade others of it. Once converting others to one's belief is seen as worthy of ridicule,[1] personal conviction must eventually become muted, while the need for an identity, which never fades, still finds satisfaction. Universal messages are in this way turned into tools that serve the purposes of individuals and identity groups, in the hope that social peace will be the consequence and reward for the effacement of those messages.

One might well wonder what it means to adhere to convictions without wanting to convince others of their truth. It seems that two levels of belief must be distinguished here. At one level, belief is a very relative and particular commitment—I believe in something that is valid for me, but that, after all, might not suit others, even had I the right to try to persuade them of its truth. This is an idiosyncratic form of believing, which strips truth of its universality and in this sense denies truth itself. Truth then becomes a statement of emotional and subjective adherence: religion, for example, finds itself explicitly regarded as an opiate. At another level, belief may refer to a universal certainty that, in the contemporary situation, must remain unexpressed in order to avoid any suspicion of proselytism. In this case, persuasion cannot occur through public conversation; it can only occur through concrete witnessing, as is historically the case under regimes that prohibit free speech. As far as religion is concerned, today, as in the first centuries of the church, only the witness, not the talker, can attest through his existence to the truth for which he stands. This situation is enough to fortify beliefs, for beliefs are meaningless unless they express a real universal, and they gradually decay as believers are replaced by those who merely pay lip service to their beliefs. One can be thankful that contemporary relativism has left only witnesses standing. Beliefs held to be certain, religious or otherwise, will emerge both purified and stronger.

If every group contents itself with assuming its identity without ever wanting to impose it on others, one might think that the result would be social harmony along the lines of a gentleman's agreement. The age of religious and ideological conflicts would be replaced by a long-lasting tolerance made possible by relativism: no group possesses the truth any more than any other.

That there are many relative points of view, however, does not in fact bring peace because relativism is by nature intolerant: it destroys the foundation on which any common discourse must be based. Under relativism, we move from one type of quarrel to another: from fighting for universals to fighting for particulars. In the society of late modernity, abuse is hurled no longer in the name of ideologies, but in the name of identities. Individuals rally around their lifestyle preferences, their cultural attachments, or their status as historical victims. I am now no longer an advocate of this or that revolution: I am young, or a Basque, or a woman, or an environmentalist.

The increased importance of particular traits does not reflect a new way of living together, but a social projection of individualism. Here groups are not communities of different and complementary people, with each working toward the common interest to the extent his means allow. Late-modern groups are rather collectives, swarms of like individuals united to defend the point of identity that is their common ground. This point of identity may be biological (sex), cultural (ethnicity), behavioral (e.g., a "wholesome, natural" lifestyle), or something else. In this sense, collectives are no more than echoes or reflections of individual narcissism at the social level. By banding together in groups of like individuals, they seek strength in numbers to support what would properly be the goals of an individual. But they do not constitute the basis for a society.

Identity collectives, united around particular modes of existence, seek no more than to root themselves ever more deeply in their particularity and to defend it against others. They affirm their way of being, the permanence of which they strive to ensure. They are the only grouping possible in a society made up of individuals. Since individuals reject complementary relationships because of the inequality such relationships presuppose, only a similarity of traits can now bring individuals together. On the other hand, in a society of person-subjects, people join groups bound together by common undertakings. Identity collectives are organized around inwardness, or origins, while open-membership groups are organized around a creative impulse and a vision of the future. The individual can ally himself only with what resembles him, because he so desperately wants equality and seeks mirrors everywhere. The person-subject accepts differences and seeks complementary relationships because he is less interested in furthering himself than in furthering a world in which he takes part.

Membership in identity groups is not based on certitudes but on historical facts: I am a woman, a Hispanic, or a homosexual. Individuals turn facts into certitudes, and then find themselves forced to invest all their speculative and emotional energy in defending the facts. This results in parochialism, in a fortress mentality, in a clinging to oneself and an overvaluing of the importance of particularity, in a provincialism that is ardently inward-looking and disdainful of the external world: in sum, in an ideology of jealousy, in the strict sense of keeping things for oneself, of hoarding, of safeguarding oneself. From this grows a static world in which everyone defends his own little patch of land, since purposeful hope has been replaced by the idolatry of origins.

Contemporary society, as an assortment of identities, reflects the diminishment of the European notion of the human being, or an extreme impoverishment of it. We see here the will to confine each individual to merely one of his allegedly vital characteristics, to assign him his place and to categorize him. Utopias limited each individual according to his age, sex, and class to the point where even specific clothes were imposed upon him. The reduction of human beings to members of a particular race or class during the past century was meant to help bring order to society, the better to govern it, and sometimes the better to reshape it.

The individual lays claim to his particularity within a larger group—a group based on an identity reduced to a single characteristic. But the person who is a subject lays claim to his uniqueness by pointing to universal referents to which he cannot be reduced. The particular is only a part of a whole; the unique is a whole in and of itself, hence the unity of the person. How will the human being be able to maintain his irreducible uniqueness, his irreplaceable nature? How will he maintain his dignity, which flows from his uniqueness? Because each person is immeasurable—and this is the source of each's dignity—no one trait can ever be the full measure of his being. The impenetrable uniqueness of the person-subject is the only thing that dignifies him. The group may provide me with an identity card, but it can never give me my personal identity, which comes from the place and role I earn within a universe of relationships.

Each of the dehumanizations that plagued the twentieth century was the product of a depreciation of the concept of man. The identity-based collectives of the contemporary age reduce man further, but in a different way. They narrow his being, because he represents much more than the trait by which he is categorized. They constrict his future and his potentialities: he is rightly destined to much more than to manifest a single characteristic. It is striking to see identity groups—particularly those who feel that they are among the victims of the old order—limit themselves to the bare minimum of their being and potential. Are women or homosexuals no more than that, fated to live their lives through the prism of this one trait, neglecting all else?

Relationships between identity groups are relationships of tolerance in its most basic form of indifference: procedures are put into place so that each can do what it pleases without interfering with others and without being judged by the others. In this way, tolerance creates a collection of individual solitudes. On its own, it creates nothing that can be shared. Identity groups divide society in two: us and them. They barely communicate with one another. How could they? For there to be dialogue, there must be a minimum of common truth. But there is none. And when *sum-bolos* disappears, *dia-bolos* appears. A "symbol" is an object broken in two, carried by two different individuals: neither half is meaningful in itself. Only the whole carries meaning, and the whole is formed only when the two halves are brought together. It is the universal that simultaneously creates bonds and carries meaning. Beyond it lies separation, *dia-bolos*.

Identity groups do not speak with each other, or rather, they communicate via invective. But a bloodless war is no less brutal for its lack of bloodshed. Hate is now fashionable, yet a society is poor indeed when its only forms of social glue are indifference and hate—especially hate, which brings radical separation into concrete expression and renders genuine interaction impossible through the destruction of a common language of beliefs and values. If the space that separates individuals is not filled, if no language based on common referents exists between them, and if the only common norm is the one according to which each lives as he likes, then the only possible interaction is violence. An identity group that considers every thought or behavior of another group to be indecipherable, because the space between them has become devoid of any meaning, will prefer violence to indifference. Unable to make the other its neighbor, it will make it its enemy. The violence in the suburbs,[2] which openly justifies itself with the words "I hate," can be traced to the existence of separated identities. Tomorrow violence will be the only form of social interaction we have, unless we re-legitimize common certainties. In this respect, hatred of the self—a general feeling of not measuring up to a common standard—engenders hatred between people. Hatred of the self masks a rejection of common cultural references. By denying them, self-hatred destroys the very ground that enables interpersonal relations.

The primary objective of contemporary society is to satisfy each of its constitutive groups, to give equal value to their particularities and also to fulfill their demands. Each must receive its share of wealth, power, and respect in a sort of quota system. But above all, each group demands laws suited to its culture or lifestyle. These demands would seem to be legitimate: if widespread agreement concerning the common good no longer exists, laws must reflect the idiosyncratic preferences of groups. The kind of organization that develops is one of "private laws," or privileges.

When Solon, in 594 B.C., gave Europe its first democratic legislation, he explicitly opposed a society of private laws. He described such laws as expressions of the will of a group having no foundation other than its own identity. Against such arbitrary norms, the majesty of the law would become a counterweight.

The descriptions of the Greek city-states of that time speak of ruthless struggles between clans, with each taking pride in its social status and the stronger crushing the weaker. "I was," said Solon, "like a wolf surrounded by a pack of dogs."

When each group can demand a norm solely for itself, a tyranny of the most powerful becomes inevitable, no matter what the word "powerful" means in any given age. Before, it was the richest group that obtained special privileges; now it is the group with the best media exposure. The law created by Solon becomes a symbol of the struggle against tyrannical aristocracies, against factions. The "law" is a bond through which a cluster of clans is turned into a society: the law becomes their "master." The citizens of antiquity knew very well that if they stopped obeying the law, they would soon find themselves again under the yoke of private arbitrariness—that is, under the non-law of the strongest.

The society of late modernity is headed in precisely the opposite direction from Solon—that is, toward the conditions of pre-Solonic times. Having banished universalist claims, it no longer knows what the law should be founded on. It therefore no longer has any reason not to satisfy the wishes of identity groups calling for particular "laws." Today, the quota system allied with affirmative action, which is in theory aimed at offsetting inequalities, comes down to identifying each individual by his group and not by personal merit. A political party needs a woman on its slate of candidates, an American university looks for a Hispanic or a homosexual to fill a job opening. What is demanded here falls short of personal merit—it is equality based on identification with a group, an equality in which the subject's autonomy is considerably diminished. I can demand a certain status because I am a woman, just as in the sixteenth century I could have demanded it because of my family name. The only difference between the two cases lies in the values affirmed by each era: in the past, blue blood, today, equality. But both then and now, the abilities and merits of the person are not the prevailing prerequisites for obtaining social power. Affirmative action does not respect the subject's autonomy unless it offers the disadvantaged the conditions they need to develop their autonomy.

The law, said Plato, refers to the universal. It seeks the good of all, which is not the addition of particular goods, but something very distantly related, in a human and mediocre way, to the good itself. "What there is in us of immortal principles" is the necessary foundation of the law, if it is to weave the social fabric and protect against arbitrariness. Although we do not have to accept the essentialism of Plato or this approach to what would become revealed law, it is true that if law is to exist as such it must transcend the preferences of particular identity groups and correspond to a common good.

Law answers both to a need for peace and to a desire to live together, which are not the same thing. The principal error of late modernity is to imagine that peace between groups is sufficient to constitute a society, or that peace between nations is the sole purpose of international life. Peace, understood as nonwar, does not make a society. Peace, taken to be its only purpose, reflects an empty society, even a nonexistent one. Society consists in bonds between individuals, not the individuals themselves as a conglomeration. It is law that ensures real peace, in the sense of peaceful living in diversity. But in addition to peace, there must be a bond. Absence of discord is not enough. There must be understanding. The very idea of law marks the intersection of both necessities.

For law to exist, one condition is indispensable: citizens must be able to give content to the common good, a content that extends beyond the particular interests of each group. This universal content—universal at least for the community in question—may be inspired by a moral code or a common religion, by an anthropology or a worldview. But it must exist for there to be law, which embodies what the citizens are to defend or undertake together.

Law is not founded on personal ties, class customs, fashions, passions, or the demands of social status or position. It is above all these things in that it is founded on realities and requirements that enable a whole society to live and ensure its survival in history. But how is a society's durability guaranteed? Should durability even be considered valuable if it is discovered to be in conflict with the desire of individuals? We no longer know how to answer these questions.

A society can never be formed from a collection of identity groups, each inhabiting its own territory. Society demands common points of reference, in which individuals and groups recognize themselves beyond their differences—like aquatic plants anchored by their roots, without which they float on the waves and disperse. Society is constituted by differences bound together by a shared foundation, by certainties concerning human existence and the paths to happiness. Living together requires a shared view of the best ways to live. But this presupposes a common understanding of human needs and ends. To stay together, then, it is not enough to proclaim, "To each his own life, and shame on he who thinks otherwise."

The law Solon imposed upon his contemporaries meant much more than positive law: its purpose was to create a world, a world common to two parties who hated each other. It proposed shared values and wove a cultural tapestry in which each member of society could find his place. Without Solon's law, there was no society, merely clan wars. A common culture, by contrast, is a structure full of meaning that reflects a society's understanding of man and his earthly existence.

Common values represent a sort of language that is constitutive of society. If each individual lays claim to his own conception of good and evil, to his own morality and law, then dialogue is no more possible than if each were to speak in his own tongue. The rejection of universal claims does not relieve us of the necessity of living in a *world*—that is, in a whole composed of meaning-bearing values. In order for a society to exist, it is not sufficient to enumerate divisive factors and then to address them one by one. Uniting factors must be determined—including the truth about man, the incomplete truth that successive ages strive to sketch anew and that expresses a world with its art and its laws, its understanding of death, its ways of doing business, even its ways of landscaping.

The common values that make up the social world show that each individual represents more than the sum of his characteristics. Common values are a language, but in the highest sense: the purpose of language is to serve not only as a *bridge*—a connection between differences, which can be likened to tolerance and the desire for peace—but also as a determination of common *meaning*. This meaning expresses a dynamic impulse, a movement. Values point to what man can become: they say that man is not yet complete, that a history awaits him.

It is only in this *world* that man finds a meaning: each person's existence is lived out as a testimony to this world. In this sense alone, personal existence is more than mere biological life. Man cannot give meaning to his life simply on the basis of his biological, genetic, sexual, or behavioral identity. To assert my identity as a woman, homosexual, or environmentalist does not give meaning to my life, except under a terrorist regime in which this identity is so oppressed, so forbidden, that it is impossible for me to be myself and, consequently, to defend a common world of any sort. In the society of late modernity, the assertion of identity is believed to suffice, erasing both the person and the subject.

Ancient European societies of the organic/holistic sort contained intermediate groups that functioned as wholes (*olos*). Each individual played a different role within a hierarchy. European holism considered the members of society as *persons*, as unique entities whose destiny was played out in interaction with others. But persons really became autonomous subjects only with the advent of modernity. Holistic society—as described, for example, by Althusius in the sixteenth century—tries to impose ends and treats personal opinion as unimaginable.

Twentieth-century totalitarianism treated those it ruled as a multitude of faceless individuals. They were not considered persons, but were denied their dignity and forbidden from developing true relationships with others. Admonitions against close family ties or close friendships were the essence of this particular form of dehumanization. Nor were individuals considered subjects. They were deprived of freedom of thought and the freedom to shape their own destinies.

Western society in late modernity is reminiscent of holism in its effacement of the subject: the individual confirms the common conscience and avoids personal responsibility.[3] It is reminiscent of totalitarianism in that it has in common the construction of collectives or masses and its weakening of the person-subject, who has trouble dealing with difference and participating in heterogeneous groups. Neither communitarian nor totalitarian, yet sharing common characteristics with both, the society of late-modern individuals is one of spontaneous gregariousness. It is merely a renewed form of the age-old phenomenon of voluntary servitude.

CHAPTER 11
ECONOMICS AS RELIGION AND THE
PARADOXES OF MATERIALISM

A general bitterness sees economism, or the preeminence of economic factors in public and social decision-making, as the triumphant ideology of the twenty-first century. This is accompanied by a sense of disgust with various connotations, a reflection in several ways of the malaise of an era.

The priority assigned to the biological body in contemporary Western societies is unequalled in history. The body—as it relates to health, sex, beauty, clothing, sports—has become the object of endless care, and requires almost exclusive attention. Our societies take a stern view of what our citizens eat and breathe and the physical risks to which they are exposed. But they show little concern for what minds digest daily in the form of televised stupidity or perversity. They applaud the enthusiasm shown by fanatics of sports, physical beauty, or relaxation. Yet they keep a vigilant and fearful eye on groups that attach their fervor to less concrete objects or projects and are quick to detect sectarian tendencies in them. While current discourse provides countless little tips on how to take care of our bodies and satisfy its needs, taking care of one's soul has never been viewed with such suspicion as now.

Enjoined to defend neither his beliefs nor his culture, nor any spiritual values, the man of late modernity is passionately interested in virtually no subject other than the maintenance of his standard of living. In fact, he has no choice; he is considered a fanatic if he defends any ideal besides an economic one. This single authorized passion, however, is not enough to make him happy. In spite of his efforts, he cannot quite manage to tremble with emotion when he hears the daily stock quotes. More and more people are discovering that means have replaced ends. But they refuse to admit that they themselves have helped turn ends into something shameful.

This state of affairs is nothing new. It has simply reached greater heights in our time. It represents the most advanced phase of modern democracy as described by Tocqueville. Based on tolerance and, more profoundly, on the equal value of all opinions, democracy seeks to prevent the development of certitudes, which generate conflict. On the other hand, it promotes the one value that receives widespread acceptance, that of material and biological well-being. Who could reject the goals of comfort and health? Since religious beliefs and social or political undertakings result in wars, it is better to rally around more prosaic and self-evident certitudes that no one can question. Democratic societies very naturally encourage economic endeavor. Any more elevated activity seems to be a sublimation or artificial exaltation, and sublimation is oppressive. And so the preservation, admiration, and beautification of the biological body become an obligation for democratic man. Any belief that proceeds in the name of the care of the soul necessarily interferes with this admiration and so seems like an insult, the seed of discord and struggle. Thus, each of us may destroy his own life or that of others if it is done in the name of physical well-being: hence the fight for euthanasia. Yet if one were to take it upon oneself to place an existential ideal ahead of the defense of biological life, one would be considered a monster: witness the opprobrium heaped upon the youth leader who dares to have his charges take physical risks in an adventure designed to forge character.

In the desert created by the disappearance of universal values and any sense of collective life, only one end is ultimately left standing—that of living well in the greatest comfort imaginable. This economic purpose is primary, for one must live before anything else; and it quite naturally rapidly monopolizes everything else, if there is nothing to compete with it. Strip man of all his ideals, ridicule the symbols that constitute his cultural world, persuade him that he has nothing to hope for or venerate, and he will worship the products of his daily life. He will channel all his enthusiasm, if he is enthusiastic, into improving it further. Persuade him that he is alone and self-made, that he owes nothing to his ancestors, descendants, spouse, fellow citizens—in short, nothing to anyone—and he will stand in front of his mirror and devote himself to the care of his own personal comfort. It would be hypocritical to blame him for this. The triumph of economism has already been guaranteed, since derision is cast upon any values that might be able to stand up against it or even to occupy a part of its territory. With the devaluation of all things unmarketable, the market becomes the sole climate of existence.

The victory of economics is also ensured, this time positively rather than by default, by the spirit of accounting that permeates and ultimately comes to inspire most interpersonal acts. Decisions that involve feelings and emotions, like choosing a spouse or conceiving a child, are increasingly colored by a bean-counting mentality. One weighs and calculates, works out prospects and compares advantages. Only a spirit of trust, generosity, and risk-taking in personal life can lead the individual out of the religion of economics in social life. In this respect, individualism as sacralization of the self gives rise to economism: the constant desire to obtain the greatest advantage for oneself encourages an accounting mindset in all one's interactions with others. It is not possible to worship oneself and to be disinterested, because disinterest involves exposing oneself to risk—sometimes for nothing in return. An individualistic upbringing, which teaches that interpersonal relationships are calculated and temporary commitments, produces adults for whom everything is a transaction.

The rejection of economism would seem then to signal a recognition of the errors of late modernity. In many cases, however, this rejection has a distorted meaning. The indignation seems directed against "the reign of king money," but that is not its focus. The greater causes of concern are the inequalities generated by unleashed economic activity. The monopoly on life held by material reality and economic well-being troubles no one when this well-being is shared. In France, Sweden is considered to be a sort of paradise because wealth is shared by everyone, even though Sweden is a country where concern for well-being has practically eclipsed freedom of thought. And the sociologists tell us that the French hold their publicly funded health care and pension system more dear than the right to vote.

This rejection of economism is not a condemnation of the monopoly of matter to the detriment of mind. On the contrary, it marks a condemnation of persistent and growing inequality in the only domain that counts: the material world. "Economic horror" does not mean that quantifiable, material goods have become relativized; on the contrary, it means they have become sacralized.[1]

Our societies claim to desire solidarity, and that is where they invest their moral idealism. They thereby believe that they are above the vulgar law of profit. However, their very solidarity is anchored in a context in which material reality is given primacy. What democracy, at least in France, is really looking for is not so much solidarity as a way of life but rather equality as a final result. Solidarity as a way of life is a constant exchange of words and gestures, of symbols and values both material and immaterial; it aims to satisfy human needs while at the same time creating human bonds. Solidarity represents the very atmosphere of a world of exchanges, and not merely a means—the most effective means possible—for redistributing goods. We seek not so much this uninterrupted exchange, experienced as a relationship with others, as we do a *solution* to the problem of inequality. We want to share and be done with it rather than to *live* in the context of relationships that sharing presupposes. However, when it comes to the intangible and unquantifiable values of the spirit, equality of distribution is extremely difficult. That is why the egalitarian spirit attempts to discredit whatever cannot be quantified. All this undoubtedly points to why economic solidarity is the only value that is accepted without debate. The individual can live as he wishes, and the only duty forced upon him is to share wealth, as if money were the only real value. It is, in fact, the only value that can be understood and equitably distributed, so much so that extraeconomic factors count for nothing in attempts to understand social problems. Economic circumstances are cited to explain family crises: crimes are caused by poverty, or if a crime can be linked to abuse, the abuse itself is caused by poverty. The inadequate parenting ability of some mothers and fathers is generally attributed to lack of money. And so, the problem of the suburbs is believed to be solvable by pouring in vast sums of money—a strategy that has proven ineffective over the years. It would be more effective to emphasize training for parents and, as a complement, continuing education through intermediary associations. But such education cultivates nonmonetary values—it teaches a sense of the meaning of life—and therefore seems suspect. Dominant opinion indicts capitalism in a way that is ultimately hypocritical, like a hospital that does not give a damn about charity. As the Brazilian philosopher Olavo de Carvalho has so correctly observed, "The capitalists proclaim that the only good is wealth, the socialists answer back that the only evil is poverty."[2]

Thus, solidarity does not even offer a way out of the narrow and arid framework of economism, since it is understood almost exclusively as the sharing of wealth. The underlying attitude of authentic solidarity—a fervor to strive for an always unachievable ideal in human relationships—has been distorted into nothing more than a desire to share possessions equally through anonymous mechanisms. Outside of the national context, it is clear that Europeans take little interest in Europe unless it aims to become a "social Europe," which is to say, a community in which the sharing of material goods and their associated advantages is established.

It is as if the essential part of common existence, the part really worth defending together, has taken refuge in the economy as the kingdom of matter. The Christian creed was, "Love and do as you please"; now we have, "Share your money and do as you please."

The passion for equality has extended its reach in unexpected ways, since it has made giving seem suspect by establishing a form of sharing that is technical and impersonal, a solitary solidarity that eliminates human relationships and takes interest solely in the result. In the process of giving, the recipient naturally feels an obligation to the giver; in other words, a material inequality is alleviated by the act of giving. But at the same time a psychological inequality is created by the feeling of inferiority that the gesture induces in the recipient. The welfare state responds to precisely this contradiction by anonymously distributing the manna from tax revenues, so that no one on the receiving end feels an obligation to anyone on the giving end.

Avoiding the inequality between giver and recipient breaks the relationship between them. Each individual ultimately finds himself cut off from others, like Leibniz's monad, which has "no windows through which anything could come in or go out." Each is connected only to a superstructure—in the individual's case, the welfare state— that feeds or taxes him. Equality is maintained, but at the cost of a broken relationship. In the realm of human bonds, only genuine friendship implies equality. All other relationships are unequal, that is, they entail giving that sometimes goes unreciprocated. No common world is possible without the acceptance of inequality. Our current system of impersonal sharing, which passes for solidarity, is destroying the common world. It is largely because of this fact that young people are eager to join humanitarian organizations where sharing takes on a human face and initiates a connection that gives a legitimacy that cannot be measured in tons of rice. To see solidarity purely in accounting terms is to accept a form of inhumanity.

International events corroborate this in a dramatic way. The now familiar phenomenon of global fragmentation is due to several factors, but in part to what has been called economic regionalism.[3] In the Girondist or federalist countries (for example, Spain and Germany, respectively), the wealthy regions grudgingly pay for the poorer ones. In Belgium, Flanders no longer wants to financially support Walloon; in Germany, Bavaria balks at having to pay for the eastern Länder. However, Flanders, until the 1960s, and Bavaria, until the late 1980s, were the beneficiaries of federal equalization payments. Why does northern Italy want to abandon the too-costly south? Why did the Czechs seem so satisfied to leave the Slovaks to their fate? Why do so many French consider Corsica too expensive? And why does South Korea fear taking back North Korea? Because material values have become essential to the point of overriding all others.

The overwhelming importance attached to GDP and the ranking of nations solely in economic terms fuel division and separation, the wealthier regions growing weary of supporting the less wealthy. This weariness, however, only makes sense in the context of a general disdain for giving itself, because giving always brings inequalities to light. Not only is it believed that giving should no longer be compensated in terms of power, recognition, influence, or in a transfer of intangible values; the act of giving meets with sharp criticism on the sole ground that it allows the giver to feel superior. At the national level and especially in France, visible charity is perceived as deliberately reminding the recipient of his inferiority. He who pays to help someone else is no longer thanked but insulted, because he allows his superiority to be displayed. For example, in Germany the eastern Länder protest that they are being colonized by "Western values." In different, less historically significant circumstances, the western Länder would undoubtedly be tempted to end their financial aid.

On the international scene, as at the national level, the poorest regions prefer to receive subsidies from the IMF or from the European Union, for these are anonymous authorities to which no obligation is felt, rather than neighboring countries or provinces. To receive aid from the latter would create relationships of inequality. The end result is balkanization due to indifference, not only through the sudden development of selfishness, but because the inegalitarian foundations of solidarity are no longer accepted.

In this context appear societies in which individuals—or regional or national groups—have difficulty accepting the idea of receiving. They wish instead to simply *collect* their due. To receive does not really make sense in a world where everyone considers himself self-sufficient by right: inequality is considered an injustice. Everyone demands that basic justice be done him, and this is why giving has lost its meaning.

This explains why the rejection of the doctrine of the "survival of the fittest" manifests itself today only in the economic realm. With this rejection we call for limits and norms. We want the state to force economic agents to assume their responsibilities. We become indignant when the mighty tread on the weak in the marketplace. Yet the law of the jungle upsets us very little in noncommercial areas: the PACS institutionalizes the irresponsibility of adults toward their children. By so carefully choosing when to protect the weak, we acknowledge the consecration of material values.

No relationship can be established without acknowledging the finiteness of being. A self-sufficient being would not need anyone and would remain solitary and happy in his own completeness. The structure of the common world is defined by giving, and giving in return, in response to the needs, inadequacies, and dependencies by which finite beings are characterized. Every human relationship begins with a need that one is willing to see filled. This is not a matter of finding a permanent solution for an abnormal or unjust situation with the goal of achieving self-sufficiency or "normality." The first condition of a "society" is the acknowledgment of our constitutive insufficiency. I cannot build relationships if I do not recognize my own need, conceived not as an exceptional circumstance or an injustice awaiting redress, but as a substantial quality. This sense of finiteness is what creates a common world and at the same time gives it meaning.

As soon as he rejects giving, the contemporary individual ceases to accept his status as a dependent person and inheritor, bound to the groups in which he is a member for better or for worse. But at the same time, he stops seeking to be an authentic subject. To consider every inequality an injustice is to view as worthless the autonomy of the subject, who creates himself through his actions. The very result of his autonomy, in terms of success or enrichment, becomes something abnormal or shameful. The individual who expects to receive his subsistence from the state is no longer a subject.

However, today's biting criticism of the predominance of the market does not have its source in egalitarian materialism alone, or even in resentment against the liberalism and capitalism that won the fight against collectivism. Nor does it proceed only from hatred toward the rich as a class enemy, still standing after the defeat of the systems that were designed to destroy it, or from a late but still hardy expression of the utopian desire to do away with the market and the economy itself. Rather, these criticisms also reflect a desire to leave the ideologies of self-sufficiency behind us once and for all. To affirm that matter and material well-being are not sufficient, having so recently acknowledged that a perfect society is impossible, is to refuse to replace one utopia with another. It is to seek a way out of the dream of re-creating man—a new man, free and unanxious at last, satisfied by health and physical well-being. To reject the religion of the market also reflects, *a contrario*, indignation involving the idea of value: in other words, it reflects the understanding that humans can, after all, give value to more than just material things, and the worship of money, even if equally distributed, diminishes them.

Otherwise stated, we have created "market democracies" on the rubble of the century's totalitarianisms. But market democracy itself is not enough for us. Does this not mean that nothing can be enough for us? Just as the establishment of democracies freed us from ideological regimes, the acknowledgment of insufficiency frees us from the ideological mindset in which we were still ensconced and into which we were lulled, for example, by descriptions of liberal democracy as "the end of history."

Here the rejection of economism considers notions of self-sufficiency to be gross deceptions. The emergence from dreams of utopia thus signals a return to age-old reflections on the human condition: "But man, despite his riches, does not endure; he is like the beasts that perish."[4] Consequently, the human situation can once again be seen as what it always has been, although we tried to ignore it: as an inadequate situation. We are guests on the earth and will never be completely at home here. Human history has nothing in common with Ulysses' voyage, at the end of which the hero goes home to familiar surroundings and loved ones, who are always there when needed and who never disappoint. The hope that we can nurture is not that we might achieve perfection, whether through a classless society or material well-being for all, but that we might manage to live better within our paradoxes. The contempt voiced toward societies in which the economy reigns supreme reminds us of the poverty of man when he is obsessed with *things,* of his inherent inability to be happy when his horizons are limited to the objects of his well-being. This contempt protests that an accounting mentality is not enough for us. It thus brings into question a life lived merely in the present and in the absence of meaningful undertakings.

The opposite of possession, the enjoyment of things, is fervor, which involves embracing values and purposes. Fervor is dispossession; it accepts in advance the fact that it can never hold in its grasp the object it seeks. The primacy given to the economy today is better understood when we recognize how scarce fervor has become. The ideologies of the twentieth century described the future world as a work of reason; Hannah Arendt has shown how they sought to substitute construction for action. The ideologues believed that achieving social happiness was a matter of gaining its possession—the happy society would one day appear in its entirety, as though it were an object, a finished and completed thing. Once this expectation was revealed to be unrealistic, the drive to possess remained the only drive possible; it had become everyone's mindset, their familiar pattern of thought. The economy thus became sacred, like it had been in the collectivist society before it, because it had become impossible to adopt a system or way of life without turning it into an idol. This is very much why the transition from one system to another, from the communist ideal to a passion for the market, happened so easily for the former communist elites in Eastern Europe. They could hardly replace ideology with religion or a moral code, for that would entail replacing possession with fervor, a complete reversal in thinking. So they naturally substituted the goal of wealth for the classless state. The two are less dissimilar than they appear, because both are things to be produced here and now; both are capable of existing in their completed form as finished objects, with no view toward the infinite.

Nevertheless, the task before us now is not to replace one idol with another, but to replace an ideological mentality with the recognition of finiteness. This radical change gives rise to a second version of anti-economistic thought. The first version does not go beyond materialism because it continues to express being in terms of having. It distorts spiritual goods by treating them as though they were material goods, still imagining them as things to be produced. This results in solidarity being seen as a circumstance to be put into effect and not as a life lived in sharing. The second version seeks to put the economy back in its subordinate place in order to allow spiritual goods to regain their rightful and unique position.

Only an attitude of fervor, which entails defining an undertaking that is by nature never completed, is capable of pursuing anything other than economic ends. Yet to the mind that has faith in nothing, that sees nothing in the universe but material things and that thinks all values are sublimations of matter, a sense of fervor remains foreign. It remains mired in the thick atmosphere of things—the only atmosphere where its particular bent of mind, habits, and background find comfort. That this atmosphere should seem too narrow should surprise no one. But the mind without faith will be able to expand that atmosphere only by profoundly changing its way of conceiving the world.

The path of possession unfolds across space, while the path of fervor unfolds across time; each determines its own dominion, so to speak. Space is king in economistic societies; the reach of each individual extends across the entire planet through instantaneous communications; each lives in nearly abolished time, just as he lives in nearly infinite space. It is no surprise that a passion for nature, which is space par excellence, is one of the only remaining passions in societies of possession, and that in such societies pantheism is replacing the religions of eternity. For ecology is a lyricism of space and pantheism a faith in divinized space: pantheism, in the form of deep ecology, is merely an extension of ecological principles. We flee from the future and invade every space, believing we can compensate for the loss of time by owning space and replacing the future with expanse. Because our temporal finiteness is naturally unacceptable to us, we make the eternity of the instant seem real by attempting to inhabit space exclusively, by seeking a boundless territory where our deficiencies are not noticeable—which is a fraud, since becoming is our way of existing. Stewardship of the earth as the setting for a futureless place is a delusion, for this expanse must be filled with projects and meaningful values. We are creatures for whom the future is not enough, for whom a hopeful prospect is also necessary. While material well-being is anchored in the space of objects and products, the figures of the spirit are written in time: in points of reference, values, ideals, plans. This temporal landscape is also where we feel at home. Contempt for economism reflects a dissatisfaction with life lived in the present: the individual living in the fleeting present can be nothing but a materialist, for spiritual values inhabit time.

Space divides, while time unifies. The sharing of an object makes it smaller, while values and ideals grow as they are shared. To share means two different things: "to share an inheritance" is not "to share a common goal." Sharing in the first sense means to divide, to cut into pieces, to distribute the different parts. The fruits of economic growth are shared in a way that enables everyone to have his share. In the second sense, sharing means the opposite: to be part of an indivisible whole. Economic wealth is distributed in portions that are proportionally smaller as the number of inhabitants increases. A spiritual or moral value grows if the number of people defending it rises. That is, possession uses and depletes wealth, whereas a spiritual value is spread by the fervor of those who adhere to it. In a society where a passion for money and economic growth dominates, goods are always too scarce and envy becomes the dominant emotion. Individuals eye each other acrimoniously, since whatever the one has, the other by definition does not possess. In contrast, when the meaning of existence is shared, interpersonal understanding develops. In a society where certain spiritual certitudes remain, at least these values belong to everyone in common: everyone can admire cultural monuments or meditate upon common ideals without depriving someone else. Each one's admiration for this society's beliefs and values nourishes the other's.

The distribution of economic goods, when it represents the only social "ideal," builds nothing that can be shared: it instead establishes a collectivity of equals deprived of interrelationships and condemned always to want more. The wealthiest are ridden with jealously and the poorest with envy. At the close of the Roman republic, writes Claudia Moatti, observers were disheartened to note that a race for material wealth was under way, and that this preoccupation permeated the city: "At the end of a spectacular reversal, the economic had won out over the political."[5]

The existence of a common world is irrevocably conditioned by the existence of shared spiritual values. The common world of the Roman republic took root in shared certitudes: "dignity, authority, prestige, and friendship"[6] were "goods" thought to transcend the individual, universal goods (at least in that society), and not just "values" left to each individual's discretion. Once individuals stop defending and upholding the ideal of these shared referents, they begin to care only about their own interests. Economics overpowers all other considerations, its reign paving the way toward social fragmentation.

A human society, when it develops authentic bonds and solidarity, finds their sources in politics and religion, which convey shared meanings. The common world is the *res publica* or *religio*, no matter how widely the contents of these terms have varied throughout history. The waning of one can in some cases be compensated by the waxing of the other: in Rome, the birth of the Christian religion reintroduced bonds that the fall of the republic had undone; after the French Revolution, the Republic rebuilt the social fabric that ebbing religion could no longer sustain. On the other hand, economics fosters separation, whereas politics fosters association. Economic, material values are counted and numbered, a requirement for individual ownership. Political values are spiritual in the broad sense that they cannot be valuated or counted, and are meant to create association: solidarity, responsibility, and justice are the requirements for understanding.

One might well ask, however, from where common values might originate. There are those who strongly believe that the demise of shared worldviews and collective undertakings, subsequent to the debacle of twentieth-century ideologies, imprisons us in the simple present. Yet there is no objective reason for collective undertakings to disappear, unless society were to have no reason to hope. But this is obviously not the case: one need think only of the energy the French people could bring to bear if they were to decide together to do something about the problem of education. In fact, the ephemeral individual merely puts on a show of self-sufficiency, pretending that there are no more collective ventures to be undertaken, because he is so terribly afraid of the risk and uncertainty of these spiritual or political goals, which are nested in time instead of space. He settles comfortably into material reality because it is objective and does not ask for the risk of belief. In the possession of a material good, there is the certainty of having fully acquired it: I *know* scientifically that a healthy chicken raised in France will keep me healthy. On the other hand, I have to *believe* in spiritual or political values—autonomy, commitment to one's word, solidarity as interrelationship. These cannot be consumed, but must be pursued over the long term and at some risk, that is, in uncertainty, starting with the uncertainty of how they are defined.

The weakening of the ability to believe gives rise to the ephemeral individual and the materialism that defines him. He claims to be self-sufficient, to immediately possess and absorb anything he lacks, in order to avoid falling prey to the dangers of belief. Human self-sufficiency, however, is by nature an imposture—which is precisely what the contempt for the religion of economics conveys. We are the brothers of Bernard Marx, Huxley's anti-hero. The Brave New World is a society devoted to perfect happiness achieved through total material well-being, a well-being that excludes the thankless uncertainty of hope. What is particular to this world is its satiety, acquired at the cost of lasting feelings, passion, and heroism—in other words, of everything that makes us human. Yet the inflexibility of self-sufficiency allows a dull anguish to show through: Bernard Marx has a feeling that humanity has been denatured by the eradication of need. That is why Nicolas Berdiaeff, quoted in the epigraph of the novel, writes, "Utopias seem to be easier to bring about than was once believed. And we now find ourselves confronted with an extremely troubling question: how can we prevent them from becoming our definitive reality?"

Our societies have something in common with the utopias of modernity: their absence of hope. But the absence of hope does not mean that happiness has finally been achieved. The deceptiveness of believing that perfection can be achieved is expressed today in economism, which seeks to bring about a utopia of material well-being. To recognize the fraud is to bring it under control, because it only remains in effect because of the false image it projects. But once the imposture has been exposed, it must be replaced. The rejection of economism has an answer in the form of a renewed appreciation for the political and the spiritual and a commitment to the goods associated with time. We remain stuck in the middle of the ford because we fear that answer. What escapes the material world goes by the name of grace—or gratuitousness, uncertainty, promise, the impulse to take a chance, sometimes even pointlessness. If man wants to do more than just count, he must believe.

CHAPTER 12

HUMAN RIGHTS, BODY AND SOUL

The materialism evident in the contemporary obsession with economic considerations and in the criticism of that obsession reveals late modernity's redefinition of *what really counts*, a redefinition that reflects late modernity's rejection of moral certitudes—religions and ideologies—as vehicles of violence. The discourse of certitude, marked by the universal, all too easily led to affirmations like *Fiat justitia, pereat mundus*. This can be translated variously (according to the context) as: may everything perish as long as we achieve real equality (Babeuf, Lenin); may everything perish as long as we achieve a pure race (Hitler); may everything perish as long as we keep our faith (Christian fanaticism) or our religious law (Muslim fanaticism). Otherwise stated, to different degrees and in different ways, by nature or by distortion (depending on the qualities attributed to them), irreducible certitudes are capable of eradicating in their name the living beings through which they manifest themselves. This ever-present possibility is therefore seen as sufficient reason to question the very legitimacy of all universalist claims and narratives.

In order to prevent the spread of belief systems that might once again give rise to fanaticism and intolerance of all sorts, we seek to be the defenders of a single simple certitude: we want to protect human beings from the terror that might be unleashed by their beliefs. Against the various creeds—may all perish, as long as we have this hope or that faith—we affirm, *a contrario,* may all faith perish, as long as man does not perish. This affirmation itself rests on a certitude, that of the value of man. Filled with legitimate anger over the destruction caused by ideals, we strike them down and establish as our sole goal the protection of what they have destroyed, namely, humanity.

The primacy of the individual over any universal is the governing principle of late modernity: may everything perish as long as man remains. In other words, to make our sole certitude a belief in the dignity of man in the singular would be to ensure the impossibility of any kind of oppression. We would thus endow ourselves with a pure truth above all suspicion.

The list of higher values in the name of which our ancestors blithely sacrificed human life would be long. The Christians of the Middle Ages committed massacres and risked their own lives to take back the Holy Land. Rulers throughout the world raised armies in order to acquire territory. The great empires sacrificed promising generations in order to consolidate power. Millions and millions sacrificed their lives as witnesses to or martyrs for a myth, religion, utopia, idea, culture, or hope. The current aim is simply to protect the physical being of today's humanity. We refuse to sacrifice humans to their gods, moral ideals, communities, or ideologies. We refuse to sacrifice earthly man for the sake of heavenly man, like fanaticized religions. We refuse to sacrifice present man for the sake of future man, like millenarian ideologies.

Today, anyone who studies key issues with a view to what the future might hold asks, What, for us, is a life-or-death issue? For one does not produce weapons without knowing for what they are going to be used. Territory or power are no longer life-or-death issues—human beings are. When we saw Milosevic preparing to deport groups of humans in order to maintain his sovereignty over a place and its culture and history, this hierarchy of values left us indignant. We now refuse to accept that people should be killed to take back Alsace-Lorraine, the Vendée, or holy lands. Why would anyone risk his life for such a thing—for nothing, since life itself represents the highest possible value?

This kind of human-rights thinking, then, might be the only truth incapable of giving rise to fanaticism, for it protects the very thing fanaticism always ends up sacrificing. Our age, in this sense true to itself, clings to the only certitude that can prevent it from committing various abuses against humanity. Our age lowers its expectations in order to protect those who could be destroyed if those expectations were higher. It refuses to speculate about the unknown or hold out impossible hopes for mankind, which might otherwise be sacrificed to this unknown or these impossible hopes. It refuses to protect beliefs, values, or places at the cost of human blood. War itself must result in "zero casualties."

How could we not admit it as a self-evident truth that a territory is worth less than its inhabitants? That an idea reminiscent of Moloch that calls for the immolation of its followers or enemies immediately loses its credibility? That the life of a single man, according to a clear-cut hierarchy, is worth more than a border, more than the glory of a few or even everyone, more than any idea, because ideas are always abstract? He who cuts Iphigenia's throat on the altar of military salvation is a barbarian ignorant of any scale of values. As a human being, I take on such importance that nothing else can hold a candle to me. Shame on those who considered the possession of Alsace-Lorraine more important than the lives of young mutineers.

And yet . . . what is left of man if we take away his territory, his culture, his religion, his ideals of liberty and justice, and even his dreams of utopia and glory? What is left is his biological life: "better red than dead." By devaluing our place and dreams, movements and thoughts, passions and desires, in order to spare ourselves from defending them at the cost of our blood, we reduce the subject to defending his last little possession—specifically, his blood, his body, and the comfort that goes with them. If he cannot feel a connection to his culture in the broad sense, both in time and space, and therefore cannot see himself as responsible for it and serving it, man is no longer anything more than a *Sapiens* with strong emotions. As the defender of himself and his offspring, he has no other purpose.

Thus, human-rights thinking in late modernity voluntarily forbids itself many hopes. It becomes short-sighted. In an effort to protect man from inhumanity, it gives rise to a cramped concept of humanness. Valued above all that transcends him in cultural time and space, the human being undergoes a radical metamorphosis. When man as biological entity represents the ultimate purpose of collective existence, the individual finds himself stripped of everything that might serve as a locus of meaning and hope. He sees himself deprived of a world so that he himself will not be surpassed or subjugated. For the sake of avoiding the violence that has historically accompanied meaning, we prefer an anemic view of ourselves.

This particular strain of human-rights thinking defines man as an individual separated from any aspirations or resources that transcend the needs of daily life. It leads to the defense of life understood as nature and instinct over against the human world understood as a producer of values, as a structured and life-transcending world. The zeal for nature in the raw that animates so many ecological currents of thought is an extension of the Nietszchean goal of a return to joyous barbarity, of the desire to uncivilize ourselves, to reject in ourselves that which is constructed—the universal, meaning—in order to return to spontaneous biological life. "At least animals only kill for food," one often says to emphasize the folly of humans capable of slitting each other's throats for a couple of acres of land or as a proof of whose god is the strongest. It is true that animals know no higher end than that of feeding themselves. War is always started in order to defend or conquer something to which value has been assigned. If we manage to convince our contemporaries that only the satisfaction of basic needs has value, it is obvious that we will no longer fight for anything but food. Should we then congratulate ourselves on this return to an uncivilized world? Must we rid ourselves of civilization to free ourselves from its negative effects?

What value does a biological life have when it is preserved at this price? If a people must avoid shedding blood in the defense of its values, if nothing is more sacred than biological life, then what remains of man? He is more than a piece of living flesh that fears death. We should remind ourselves that the slave is someone who prefers life over liberty. Yes, he avoids death, but for what kind of existence? The ancients said that honor consists in holding the values of life more dear than life itself. It is surely true that history has sacrificed too many lives for dubious values. But must we now go to the opposite extreme?

The human rights thinking of late modernity certainly has solved the problem of the terrorism of certitudes, but it has solved it by dramatically impoverishing those whom it wishes to protect. It gnaws at and diminishes man in order to safeguard him more fully, taking from him every space he inhabits: religion, territory, culture. A new nihilism is introduced into societies given over to fear of certitudes. The original nihilism, having grown out of the philosophies of suspicion, accused alleged truths of imposture and rejected them as arising merely out of our fears and ambitions: they were but the opiates of the people. The nihilism of late modernity pillories certitudes for the crimes against humanity they have fomented. The original nihilism was triumphant and scornful, proud of its juvenile lucidity and full of hopes for liberation. The second is disappointed and panic-stricken. With the original nihilism, the subject was empty, having rejected everything he left behind, and ready to invent new errors—which he did not waste any time in doing. In the new nihilism, the subject is empty out of precaution, and determined to remain entrenched in his emptiness.

But the cultural world in which man lives must include common certitudes. Because they are in fact dangerous, every world contains within it the permanent risk of fanaticism and oppression. This risk cannot be eradicated without abolishing the cultural world itself. This would leave a world in which man is no more than a biological being waiting to die.

What is a person, if nothing is more important than his ability to breathe? Life, the condition of existence, becomes its sole end. And in so becoming, it withers away. For if life is the condition of lived existence, existence within a meaningful world is what characterizes a *human* life. Must one *not exist* in order not to die before one's time?

Man is this animal that undertakes the adventure of meaning, an adventure that constitutes a risk. He walks on the edge of a precipice, by daring to accept the risk of error and conflict between certitudes. If he gives up out of fear of the dangers that await him, he empties himself of an invisible substance. He narrows and shrivels up. He deliberately tosses overboard a part of his civilizing heritage and mimics the passive serenity of the half-evolved animal. He thereby strips himself of his self, rejecting the dignity that is properly his own: the dignity that is his as a bearer of meaning.

The crimes perpetrated in the name of universal claims have led us into an absurd alternative: we now have to choose between adherence to redemptive universals or the protection of a body devoid of spirit. This binary thinking errs through its oversimplification. The philosophy of rights dehumanizes man when it limits itself to defending nothing more than his biological life. We would do better to defend human rights body and soul: not only human life, but the human cultural world and human certitudes. Conflict inevitably arises from face-to-face confrontation: how far may one go in order to defend a territory, a religion, a value, a way of life, or a way of thinking? All conflict cannot be avoided. It is the irreducible risk that must be accepted if humanity is to be worthy of its name.

CHAPTER 13
THE UNIVERSAL AS PROMISE

Late modernity relies on a universal certainty of its own: that human rights are valid and must be respected, with the human understood as a biological entity desirous of well-being but stripped of ideals and spiritual certitudes. In the name of respect for human rights, and only in its name, it is now permissible to raise armies. That human rights must be respected is the only truth that can justify violence, since human rights are assumed to be universal and absolute. This universal certainty thus gives itself the authority, even the duty, to interfere in the affairs of others.

Nothing, however, really indicates that we have escaped our bad old ways. Claiming to protect man himself instead of his God, his territory, or his glorious future, this universal is proving itself capable of a fanaticism similar to the universals that preceded it. It constrains and ostracizes; it spews hatred toward those who reject it. The war in Serbia in 1999 sheds considerable light on the subject. For the first time, the universal of human rights was put to the test in the most extreme of acts: war. The intervention in Serbia challenged received ideas and raised new questions. The United States and its allies attacked Serbia in order to prevent it from proceeding with its plan of ethnic cleansing in Kosovo. This was a humanitarian conflict, carried out at least publicly in the name of respect for human life. It grew out of recent history, from the shame felt in Western countries over the massacres perpetrated in Bosnia—massacres they had severely condemned but had failed to prevent by taking action early enough.

The preventive action against the Serbs was clearly in keeping with the necessity of obeying our most cherished principles. Nevertheless, as events unfolded, several disquieting questions came to the fore.

1. The issue here was to prevent violence against the population in Kosovo no matter what the motive for this violence. The Serbs' goal was to maintain under their control, by any means possible (including murder), a region they considered culturally vital. The allies were quick to equate Milosevic with Hitler because he used violence against civilians and because he killed in the name of values he believed were higher than the value of human life.

2. Nonetheless, the allies granted themselves the right to kill Serbians in the course of air attacks. In other words, only the cause of human life is worth sacrificing lives for. It would be simplistic to see a contradiction here, for the issue is to defend a cause over the long term, to set an example by killing the guilty in order to defend the innocent. Yet the allies felt that doing so somehow invalidated the morality of their actions. Unable to clearly legitimize their tactics, they spoke euphemistically of "collateral damage," thereby displaying the cold disregard they had wished to avoid. They treated their victims as things.

3. On the other hand, the allies never went so far as to risk the lives of their own soldiers. In other words, if one may in extreme cases kill to defend life, one cannot actually die for it. Must we then paradoxically believe that, in this moral war fought in the name of human life, the lives of some are worth less than those of others?

4. Another observation may help to understand the paradoxes of the previous one. The allies refused to call this conflict a "war." In

fact, war was never declared. In the minds of the allies, this was a police operation, which explains why they went to such lengths to protect their pilots. A police force that is tracking a criminal takes care not to put its officers at risk, but those officers may shoot at the criminal, whose crime immediately places him in the role of the accused. In Serbia, then, the crime was considered to be objective, as if it were defined by a statute of law: the moral law of human rights has the effect of statutory law, as if it were an official universal.

5. The situation could be compared to that of a police operation aimed at saving schoolchildren taken hostage by a sadist. The life of the sadist "counts" less than the lives of the police officers. In principle, however, the officers are willing to risk their lives for the children. In the intervention against the Serbs, however, there was nothing of the sort. The pilots risked nothing in bombing the columns of Serbian tanks on their way to Kosovar villages. The lives of the victims "counted" less than the lives of their defenders.

Must we then conclude that the Westerners would have done better to allow the Serbians to calmly cleanse the coveted provinces? Certainly not. Perhaps what should be concluded, first, is that the clear conscience of Westerners, their moralistic picture of themselves as righters of wrongs, and their hatred for Milosevic, portrayed as a fiend, all ring very false. The situation appears to be much more complex than our certitudes would have us believe. We thought that, in order to do good, it would be enough to fight evil—in this case, to fight those who killed their fellows in the name of values they claimed were higher than life itself. We believed that fanaticism could be found only on the other side. As it turns out, things are more ambiguous than that. Far from situating ourselves as unconditional defenders of human life, we found ourselves measuring the value of life according to whom the life belonged: our lives first, then the lives of the victims, and finally the lives of the assassins (if all Serbs can be included in this category, which I do not claim).

Because the question has never been openly raised, we are surprised to see ourselves caught in the act of fanaticism. This was clear in the ostracism inflicted on those in France who challenged the legitimacy of the intervention—even if they expressed their views calmly and reasonably. The defenders of human rights ended up looking like religious fanatics or ideological maniacs who have taken it upon themselves to eradicate Evil.

How can we not compare this intervention to the colonial adventures or ideological wars of the past? After shamelessly destroying Serbia, didn't we set up a new protectorate there? What difference can be established between the colonizing "mission" of Kipling, today so disgraced, and the fervor that impelled us to protect the victims of these Serbian barbarians? The difference is as follows: previously the primary reference point was European civilization, while today the primary reference point is biological life. But the approaches are similar, founded in the certainty that there can be a just use of force. Haven't the old ideologies simply been replaced by a kind of human-rights fundamentalism, no less sectarian than what it claims to be fighting against? The intervention against the Serbs clearly reveals the distorted relationship we maintain with the Good, a relationship that smacks of the old vanquished ideologies and follows in their footsteps. We believed, and perhaps still do, that the majesty of our values acquits them in advance of ever being oppressive.

In his description of human progress, Condorcet predicts that we will one day abandon our shameful missionary civilization to establish outposts from which we will spread Enlightenment to other peoples.[1] In other words, he believed that Enlightenment could be spread without oppression or the illusion of possessing the pure and objective Good—an illusion that marks all ideologies. The way in which the allies twisted words during the intervention—"war," "bombing," "civilian victims" were stricken from their vocabulary—is characteristic of the domination of a system that takes itself to be the sole criterion of the Good, then proceeds to conjure away its misdeeds by ceasing to name them.

If a war carried out in the name of a universal certitude cannot be equated with a police operation, it is because no universal can be equated with a statute of law. We cannot entirely know the Good, nor can we fully achieve it. Only this negative certitude will enable us to free ourselves of the ideological mentality. The apostles of human rights falsely believe that because their cause is good, they can do anything. However, fanaticism is to be found less in the content of any given "Good" than in the idolatry of this content, in the belief in its earthly reign and in the possibility that we can achieve it with our own hands. In other words, if the philosophy of rights is to be a new kind of universal that is respectable and not susceptible to fanaticism, it must not only value human dignity over faith, race, or class. It must above all else refuse to idolize its object.

We can recognize an objectively bad or objectively good event in extreme situations. But the positive universal that defines the Good inevitably remains insufficient. We cannot grasp anything in its totality. We can grasp only flashes, echoes, remnants of a total Good, which always remains an object of promise and faith. Our certitude, even if we clearly perceive the path it takes, remains incomplete, mixed with the finiteness that constitutes our being. We are the ones who determine its contours, we who have a history, mores, and desires steeped in the uniqueness of a time and place. This is why to impose our certitude on others is unscrupulous. The universal claims of human rights, in their concrete description, are subject to debate, because as finite beings we cannot create perfect things. During the war in Kosovo, Westerners were shocked to learn that the allied intervention had led to atrocities committed by Albanians: although victims, the Albanians were no more innocent by nature than the Serbs, who were not so diabolical that they could not become victims themselves.

We do not *possess* our certitudes. We do not have them at our mercy. We know them and serve them only insufficiently. Our actions, therefore, can never adequately achieve them. They can only be awkwardly inspired by our certitudes. The striking thing about the war in Kosovo was the clear conscience and arrogance of the righters of wrongs—the way they considered themselves the masters of moral truth.

The cause we defend may be pure, but we ourselves never are, and our cause has no defender other than us. The means we use to defend it are always debatable and subject to our weaknesses. With rare exceptions, such as open and cynical antihumanism, universal claims and shared certitudes are rarely perverse in themselves. Yet the way we use them can make them destructive. Action can distort a great cause.

Thus, the universal idea of human rights is not a tangible result, the image of a specific state of affairs to be brought about in a given society. Being incomplete, it takes the form of a promise, a locus of expectation. It is merely an object of hope. It is forever to be re-worked and reinvented. The West's mistake in Kosovo was to try to *achieve* human rights through dramatic action. But it is not in our power to do so. The universal is a direction, a path open to a Good with which we cannot equate our actions.

The universal implies, to begin with, transcendence, a stake on higher ground. Accordingly, to name a good that would suit all mankind is to take a great risk. It has as its price an earthly melancholy, which is felt at the sight of the gulf that separates the universal from its actualization. The only universal that would not succumb to the temptation of fanaticism would be the one that remained in its place, content with its status of promise, object of hope, point on the horizon. Without this distance, it sooner or later becomes a form of terrorism.

We cannot define earthly perfection. Even less can we bring it about on a large scale. Human actions represent no more than groping attempts to move closer to a good that we confusedly perceive. Human rights must remain reference points that are always in question. An event may alter their contours. Their interpretation and application depend on circumstances and situations. Mention of this dependency causes indignation in our contemporaries, who believe they have discovered a body of intangible truths. In the name of human rights, we are imitating those biblical literalists who mistake every illustration for an absolute. But an illustration provides nothing more than a picture by which points of reference come into focus in a given era.

Thus, late modernity still gives credence to the lie that there is a definable and eventually achievable Good that will establish itself with the sovereignty of domination and violently cast out everything that does not conform with it. We have not yet learned, as Jean Roy formulates it, that "the fortress of the absolute is impregnable."[2] We will never really abandon the ideological mindset unless we become iconoclasts, shattering the images of the Good that have become so many fetishes. The equality of collectivism was a fetish, and now human rights have been reinvented as a fetish. The twenty-first century will have to destroy idolized images of the Good just as the ancient iconoclasts destroyed images of God—not that they stopped believing, but they rightly saw these descriptions of God as diminishments that threatened his transcendence. The idolaters in the book of Exodus (20:4–5) prefigure the modern ideologues in their sacralization of the immanent. The texts in the Old Testament on the prohibition of idols, and Kant's writings on the human ignorance of the Good, stigmatize certain permanent temptations of human thinking, ones that returned in full force in the totalitarianisms of the twentieth century. We have yet to call them into question.

To despair of ever completely knowing the Good does not mean that it will suffice simply to destroy evil, which is easier to recognize, in order to advance History. Hate walks amid ruins; only fervor is constructive. That is why a new way of thinking the future must be found in order to move forward toward an ever incomplete representation of the Good, which is the very movement of hope. Hope is confidence in the many possible expressions of the Good.

It is, however, difficult to see how the destruction of idols could be accomplished without openness toward the spiritual. The suppression of spiritual referents is precisely what conferred on secular referents their abusive status as absolutes. The return of spiritual referents alone would make possible the destruction of idols: idolatry cannot be avoided except through the recognition of transcendence. The philosophy of rights is not a religion. But it articulates mankind's transcendence over nature (how could we possibly be subject to the impalpable and indescribable Good that nature represents?), thereby establishing humanity's intrinsic dignity. Intrinsic dignity, as a point of reference, is expressed as a horizon and a promise, forever to be defined and forever to be achieved: the eternally incomplete earthly ideal. The hope of achieving this ideal establishes us within a history waiting to be made, one that is ever rising and noncyclical, a cultural idea that is distinctively our own.

The dream of a messianic reign lingers on in our thoughts and partially shapes them. The end of messianism will come only when we have abandoned our impatience: salvation remains always incomplete. Impatience for the reign of the Good can be seen in the machinations of the Inquisition, in both the red and the brown totalitarianisms, but also in the invention of the International Criminal Court, that global righter of wrongs which has taken upon itself to purge the earth of its monsters. We will rebuild a common world only by avoiding this kind of impatience. We can struggle against evil, but we cannot pose as supreme righters of wrongs, searching out evil wherever it may be found and then eradicating it.

Just as the allied intervention in Kosovo pretended to be a police operation, the idea of an international criminal tribunal assumes that our interpretation of human rights has the status of positive law, at once objective and empowered to inflict punishment. But the very act of equating a moral universal with statutory law is inquisitorial. It indicates that Westerners believe that they have discovered natural law incarnate and have taken upon themselves the mission of imposing it on the entire world, thereby paving the way for all manner of injustices—for meting out God's law is too great a task for mere mortals.

A law is just only if it is enforced throughout the territory placed under its jurisdiction. The International Criminal Court will therefore be under the obligation to try all the criminals on the planet. Unless it does, its selection of cases will be subject to partisan considerations. This is already the case: Pinochet, yes; Castro, no. Westerners, so guilt-ridden when they think of their colonialist past, are thus in the process of organizing moral and political meddling on an unprecedented scale. The colonizers believed in the objective superiority of the civilization they brought with them, which is precisely what we reproach them for today. Although a crime against humanity is incontestable as a crime, is it possible to judge a tyrant in Borneo in the same way we would judge Eichmann? A statutory law, enforced throughout the territory of a state, makes sense because that society's members all live within a shared culture. In France's unified jurisdiction, it is difficult enough to judge Muslim genital excision as mutilation. A natural law forbidding crimes against humanity. does exist. Yet it is less certain that it is up to us to officially apply that natural law, to be the architects of its transformation into universal positive law.

Who are we to judge all peoples in such a fashion? Who are we to believe ourselves capable of checking the impunity of crimes around the globe? Only a plurality of laws and lawmaking states can compensate for our unworthiness to judge. Plurality is the lone guarantee against the human temptation to play the divine righter of wrongs. If there is only one court left on earth, one that rises above all others, it will quickly turn into a court of public opinion, into a divinely inspired authority—with the people themselves having taken the place of God.

The verdict of popular justice is without appeal because it represents final and, in a sense, divine authority. It is accountable to no one. The people themselves deliver up the accused in the name of the pure morality they represent. International public opinion—communicated through the media, which is supposedly in close touch with the people—will deliver victims to the International Criminal Court. We are already seeing one "manhunt" described with jubilation.[3] Divine wrath is at work. It jeers at and spits on the accused while pushing him on to face the court. The accused is guilty on arrival. Hate calls the tune, because a partisan settling of accounts often lies behind the accusations. No ex-communist officials are seen fretting about their futures. Once justice takes itself for Justice, it becomes class or clan justice, for the universal is just too big for us.

What else can we do? one might ask. Bear witness. Judge crimes against humanity committed on our own soil and judge them dispassionately, without jeering and foaming at the mouth. In other words, we should first of all refuse to involve ourselves in the game of popular justice. And we should learn to forgive. Concrete good inspires people and makes them want to follow its example—unlike lecturing about the Good, which tends to be offensive. A people who behaved justly and without hate toward the murderers in its history would inevitably attract secret admiration. Instead, in the current scenario, we will provoke a reaction of revolt among the people punished by our hand; in the worst case, we will provide a justification for the very deeds we have taken it upon ourselves to punish.

We must replace the figure of the dispenser of justice with that of the just person.

The dispenser of justice and the just person are both judges, agents of judgment: their mission is to separate good from evil, to name the responsible and the guilty. The just person is just by his inner nature. The dispenser of justice acts as the machinery of justice; he *is* justice. The just person acts as nothing more than himself—his action is just and, because he acts alone, he is unarmed. The dispenser of justice believes that he is objective and that his verdicts are beyond appeal because they represent just judgment, which he believes he speaks for in its Platonic form. The just person, on the other hand, belongs to the contingent world: he adjusts to circumstance and knows that justice is man-made and therefore always insufficient.

When the Everlasting asked King Solomon what he wished to receive as a reward for his good behavior, Solomon replied, discernment. In granting Solomon discernment, God did not actually give him anything, for Solomon's very request demonstrated that he possessed it already. Solomon thereby revealed that he had perceived the core of human weakness: we must judge here on earth, yet only God can judge and God is not on earth—a terrible paradox.

Thus, the just person knows that justice is impossible. He judges because God is absent. He judges with the humility and caution of an employee who is promoted to take the place of a boss who has resigned, or with the fear of the eldest son who must assume the role of the missing father. The just person does not know what justice is, because he sees it as belonging to another sphere. But he tries, however awkwardly, to define what is just, because without it the human world would collapse into inhuman chaos.

The dispenser of justice, by contrast, believes that he holds the definition of justice itself in his hand and so decides without a second thought. He does not need discernment because he *knows*—in the same way that God will know on judgment day. The dispenser of justice eventually identifies himself with the Good, because he serves no other cause and believes that he possesses the essence of the Good.

The dispenser of justice and the just person, the fanaticized universal and the universal as promise, cannot be distinguished by the referents to which they point; rather, they can be distinguished by their relationship to their referents. The just person idolizes nothing earthly because he knows that concrete good has no recognition beyond his discernment, which he knows to be limited. This is why he prefers not to lecture others on achieving good in this world. He is like the parent of a large family who has raised his children without major damage: he will seldom boast or preach to others. Because he has had to make so many delicate decisions, the very idea of successful child-rearing seems to him a mysterious alchemy in which humility grows along with patience. A legislator may decide for good reasons that a country like France, rich with old traditions, must abandon the law of an eye for an eye and abolish capital punishment. Public opinion, however, cannot then point its hateful finger at countries that do not do the same, as if there were a visible borderline, valid in every time and place, separating laws and behavior that respect human rights from those that do not.

The past, like the present, does not come under the gavel of our final judgment. The mentality of the dispenser of justice, which too often fuels the universal idea of human rights in today's world, is visible in the phenomenon of repentance. The "duty to remember" eventually becomes the past on trial. Manichaeanism is introduced into history and every epoch becomes tainted by its crimes: Greek democracy by its slavery, the Church by its Inquisition, the colonial periods by their abuses. Ideologies treated the human past as pre-history, while we condemn it as a moral failure. The only heroes we recognize from the past are those who fought against the values of the past within that same past.

Who do we take ourselves for when we ferret out the villains of the past? Are we so perfect as to be able to judge our ancestors so carefully on the scales of justice? Our bad conscience, overwrought about the past, is coupled with a self-satisfied good conscience about the present: we never stop congratulating ourselves for having established the duty to intervene in the affairs of others, for no longer allowing crimes to be perpetrated, for having at last given women their proper place in society, and for having indicted homophobia.

Yet, it seems obvious that we will continue to change with time, and that some of our ways will seem unacceptable to our descendants. We can certainly refine and improve our behavior, but at the same time, to drag our ancestors through the mud does not indicate very sound judgment. Indeed, it bespeaks an infantile form of Manicheanism—do we really think that time stops with us? This is what the millenarians who preceded us believed. No one could ever paint a completed picture of the moral world to serve as an absolute benchmark against which we might judge history in its entirety.

There is a newspaper report that describes, complete with photos, the human beings on exhibit at the Zoological Gardens in Paris at the beginning of the twentieth century.[4] Our stomachs turn in indignation. Our gut reaction is to think of our forefathers as monsters and, conversely, to consider ourselves paragons of virtue. No one would want to adopt a historicist view and conclude that "other times had other ways," the slogan of moral relativism. Nevertheless, in the middle ground between the attitude of the dispenser of justice and that of the relativist, there is one certainty: respect for human dignity is neither a universal truth determined once and for all nor a value rooted in a time and place, but rather a universal promise, which each era must strive to articulate and achieve, a transcendence pursued within the timeframe of history.

It would seem that Europe's repentance over mass extermination has resulted in a sort of cathartic purge. Yet it is one thing to recognize one's own crime; it is quite another to extract from it a criterion for sorting the good- from the evildoers everywhere. The worst crimes have been committed by people quite like us. The terrible periods of history have been lived through by humans who gave in to Evil and sometimes even made pacts with Evil, yet it is not for us to condemn them as Satan's accomplices. The humiliation that today's Russians or East Germans feel comes from their sense of injustice: a period of time cannot be erased by decreeing it completely unredeemable; intertwined with and bound up in an era are the makings of human beings, including their very souls. The last century in Russia and East Germany saw countless butchers and victims, destroyed and terrorized lives, traitors and cowards, yet amid all this inhumanity, human beings lived. We can profit from experience by singling out the kinds of acts we no longer wish to see, but we cannot retell history in the form of a judgment from God.

Repentance is inner conversion. To understand that, one must step out of the mindset of the dispenser of justice. To change one's beliefs, to reverse oneself, is a process of the mind that owes something only to the conscience and the will. Like the process of believing, repentance cannot obey an external command or yield under an external threat. No one can force someone else to believe, as life amply demonstrates. Similarly, no one can force someone else to repent. Prevailing opinion, elevated to a form of power, is today imposing repentance under the threat of ostracism, a sign of the confusion between genuine repentance and the recognition of wrongdoing, of the equation of moral fault with scientific error. As if a moral wrong were not entirely a matter of personal conscience! The same reasoning that makes the punishment of Serbs a police operation—objective and mechanical, draped in officiality—makes a travesty of repentance, turning it into a mechanism operated by external controls. This is depersonalizing, a denial of the moral conscience and the uniqueness of moral wrong as an act perpetrated in the depths of the self and with the self as judge. Mandatory repentance is totalitarian in manner, similar to the confessions extorted during history's darkest trials. In such cases, the wrong represented a crime against the party or its ideology, against official institutions or orthodoxies, rather than a crime against the Good, which no one possesses.

The contemporary vulgate has turned repentance into a public statement conceded out of fear, a display of renunciation. This implies the ultimate negation of the subject, even his destruction, because he is cut off from the very roots of his greatness—that is, from his ability to reemerge from the muddy waters into which his wrong had plunged him. True repentance, on the other hand, means a reversal of the self that takes place in the shadows of a reflective conscience: it is to abandon and let go of the "old" self; it is the inner death of a self that has since been transformed. Repentance is possible only through the slow and painful inward journey that overturns rationalizations, accepts shame, and transforms it into a new hope. It is possible only in a culture that recognizes the importance of the individual conscience. Only the person as subject can repent and convert. When I feel shame, it is *I* who am ashamed: this is how the subject is revealed.

CHAPTER 14
THE UBIQUITY OF EVIL

The dignity of the person, that cornerstone of the philosophy of rights, is an ontological quality, a constituent part of the person's being. That human dignity should not be contingent on belonging to any group—whether social, ethnic, or sexual—is today a shared certainty. That dignity should not be contingent on an individual's moral qualities or physical abilities is, however, an obvious truth that late modernity has difficulty accepting. We are thus re-creating dividing lines, ones different from those of yesterday, between the worthy and unworthy. This is true of the dividing line between right and wrong, which was inherited from ideological thinking and hardened, in its subjective tendencies, by the magnitude of the crimes of the twentieth century.

During the Christian period of our history, we lived with the concept of "original sin." This meant that evil was shared by all human beings without exception; each had his part in it. Evil represented a kind of common heritage from which no one could claim to be exempt. Even the saint is described not as "perfect," but as someone who gropes for perfection as he moves closer to God. Religions that separate "the perfect" from the rest are deformed religions that, through a catastrophic perversion, seek to bring heaven down to earth.

In Europe, the certainty that evil is shared was not peculiar to Christianity. The two original branches of our culture agree on this point. The Old Testament relates the myth of an originary sin, the result of the freedom given by the creator to the being he created and carrying the meaning that evil is an integral part of the human condition. The Greek philosophers of antiquity, in a society that did not recognize transcendence, put forward the same postulate. Merely on the basis of his observation of human behavior, Aristotle, for example, writes that civil strife is caused by "profit and honor . . . insolence; fear; the presence of some form of superiority; contempt; or a disproportionate increase in some part of the state."[1] That is, civil strife is caused by human nature, and not by the vices of one system or another. Reflecting on social inequities, he writes, "lawsuits about contracts, convictions for perjury, and obsequious flatteries of the rich are denounced as due to the absence of a system of common property. None of these evils, however, is due to the absence of communism. They all arise from a wickedness of human nature."[2]

For antiquity as well as for Judaic and Christian thought, all humans without exception participate in good and evil. Society can therefore never be made perfect, because man is not destined to become an angel. Nevertheless, no one can be singled out as the devil incarnate: even if evil or perverse, no person, whether alone or in the company of his own kind, is the source of perversion. This source remained the locus of philosophical astonishment for the ancients, and of the original mystery of freedom for believers.

Modernity inaugurated a new interpretation of the question of evil and claimed to find a historic solution to it. Rousseau and Fichte were two major prophets of this reordering of things, which was destined to transform our entire understanding of social existence. We are still living under their aegis, probably without even realizing it.

For Rousseau, "original sin" is a deception. Man is by nature innocent and pure, as long as he has not been corrupted by culture and society. To explain this corruption, there must have been a mythic moment in time when the initial split between the innocent and the guilty appeared. He who first said, "This is mine," invented private property, and thereby signalled the advent of a group of intrinsically guilty people, responsible for the evil in the world. Rousseau, who thought of himself as the only natural and pure man to have survived perversion, predicted the eventual arrival of a group of innocents capable of re-creating the lost society. The modern understanding of scapegoating here finds its origin. A little later, Fichte firmly rejected the thesis of original sin: "It is an absurd slander on human nature to say that man is born a sinner. . . . His life makes him a sinner."[3] On those grounds, he called for the construction of a "perfect system" through the fashioning of a "perfect man,"[4] for the German people were, in his view, ontologically innocent.

The abandonment of the idea of "original sin," understood as evil rooted in our very condition, gives rise to two consequences: it becomes possible to hope for the elimination of evil, and it becomes necessary to situate the cause of evil somewhere else. A declared belief that evil can be eradicated from the face of the earth raises the question of how to accomplish this task of secular redemption. The only possible solution consists of isolating evil in certain groups—both visible and recognizable—which can then be eliminated. The founding folly of the twentieth century, latent in the philosophical candor of Rousseau and Fichte, lies in the certitude that elimination of the bourgeoisie, or of the Jews, would at last open the way for a free, just, and peaceful society.

Scapegoating can be seen as the predominant mental process of the modern age. In the old Christian society, the "good" were distinguished from the "bad" on Judgment Day. The modern ideological separation between the innocent and those responsible for evil reflects, perhaps, a secularization of the distinction between heaven and hell. It is an eminently dangerous secularization, since it then becomes possible to single out some human beings as unworthy, as radically separated and therefore exposed to the radical contempt of the dispenser of justice. At any rate, this continuity shows just how strong the temptation always is to answer the question of evil by singling out a scapegoat. The Christian vision of hell is for similar reasons questioned by certain theologians for its Manichaeanism. Gehenna may very well involve not the whole of each guilty person but the guilty part of each person.[5]

The totalitarian systems of the twentieth century were thus made possible only by a Manichaeanism that splits humanity in two. The attempts to negate original evil and to create the perfect society mutually sustain each other. The former makes the latter possible, and the latter requires the former, for the will to create a society without blemish runs up against the undeniable existence of Evil. It then becomes necessary to explain why the present state of society is corrupt—a strange fact if humanity is indeed innocent. Institutions are therefore held responsible. Yet behind the institutions are flesh-and-blood human beings. The real culprits then become those who built these structures, those who justify them, those who live off them, or those who perpetuate them. With implacable logic, the presumption of original innocence, combined with the existence of concrete evil, engenders a moral Manichaeanism. Certain groups will become intrinsically guilty, while all others will remain intrinsically innocent. This barbarous dichotomy results in the creation of what are termed subhumans, or "insects," forever responsible for the evil in the world. As Solzhenitsyn wrote, "Lenin proclaimed the common, united purpose of 'purging the Russian land of all kinds of harmful insects.' . . . It is not possible for us at this time fully to investigate exactly who fell within the broad definition of *insects*. . . . People in the cooperative movement were also insects, as were all owners of their own homes. There were not a few insects among the teachers in the gymnasiums. The church parish councils were made up almost exclusively of insects, and it was insects, of course, who sang in church choirs. All priests were insects—and monks and nuns even more so. . . . [T]here were indeed many insects hidden beneath railroad uniforms. . . ."[6]

The fall of totalitarian regimes should have precipitated the end of scapegoating. For that to have happened, however, it would have been necessary to substitute a new worldview for the previous one. This was not to be. The foundations of contemporary thought remain those of the same revolutionary modernity that gave rise to totalitarianism. Evil in the world has not found any other explanation. The question of why it exists remains. It still makes no sense. And so it must be located within a group whose wickedness is sufficient explanation. The torturers and executioners of yesteryear are ready-made targets. The portrayal of the Nazi in films and in the print media is a clear example of this personification of the abominable: he is without humanity and, it seems, without weakness, seamless in his total cruelty; there is nothing finite about him. He is nothing but the magnitude and cunning of his crime— in other words, Lucifer himself. In this portrayal, we delineate a humanity without humanity; we focalize absolute evil and at the same time absolve all others. Pierre Assouline describes the Manichaean figure in his novel *La Cliente*,[7] which tells the story of a young man who decides to track down a traitorous woman who was an informer in the Vichy era, taking himself for the eye in the tomb of Cain. Is he so blameless that he alone can bring about justice, like the Everlasting on Judgment Day? He thinks he is innocent, which is only natural, since the other, the guilty one, embodies all evil, *is* absolute evil. Assouline's hero is contemporary man; our society is teeming with dispensers of justice who separate the good from the bad of bygone eras without the shadow of a doubt. They denounce, stigmatize, seek to inflict punishment, and nurse feelings of hate, always in the domineering and sententious tones of the prosecutor. The dispenser of justice *is* justice, not because he is sure he recognizes inhuman behavior—everyone would agree with him—but because he thinks he recognizes an absolute and therefore monopolistic personification of evil. The hero in *La*

Cliente himself remains a prisoner of the original postulate of the system he rejects: a ravaging Manichaeanism that leaves him presumably innocent and pure. Near the very end, however, the circumstances surrounding the informant's deed are revealed to him. The hero is then plunged into an abyss of perplexity—not that the circumstances excuse the act, but the accused reveals the same fears, sufferings, and cowardly weaknesses that the accuser recognizes as his own. The accused takes on a human face. The young man's hate gives way to painful reflections. Although the seriousness of the crime is not questioned, a common world is reestablished.

Manichaeanism is the architecture of reduction. In order to categorize, one must resort to abstraction. The guilty person is reduced to an act taken out of its context; she becomes defined by a crime that then exclusively identifies her. The complexity of human action is denied. The mere act of creating an abstraction makes hate possible, for by simplifying, it leaves only the evil intact. When crimes are resituated in the context in which they were committed, criminals can be seen in all their vulnerability and, consequently, in their dignity. It is striking to see how in contemporary France a whole generation has moved from historicism—every act is justified by its context—to Manichaeanism—judgment is absolute and must not take context into account. In both cases, the freedom and complexity of the person as subject are denied. In the latter, the person is reduced to an act that presumably determines him entirely; in the former, the person is denied his act and his responsibility because he is governed by circumstance.

The human being, an enigma for the ancients and a mystery for Christians, remains irreducible to categorization, whether moral or social. In this world there are neither demons nor angels; no man embodies the quintessence of Evil or the quintessence of Good. No executioner is entirely evil, no victim entirely innocent. Essences escape us. We remain a mysterious mixture, forever more complex than the categories into which we slip. The very idea of *person* expresses this infinite complexity: a fathomless well, impenetrable thickness, which no one can reduce to an act or trait, any more than to membership in a particular group. This is why Eichmann was provided with a lawyer. Ceausescu was executed without a lawyer, because his judges belonged to the same totalitarian system as did he. When democracies equate Milosevic with Satan, with all the requisite pathos of hate, and themselves take on the role of angels of the Good, they have forgotten the mystery of being, the complexity of the enemy as a person, and their own finiteness. The philosophy of rights has then deviated from its meaning.

All forms of Manichaeanism produce hate, and all the more so when based on moral criteria. They then place the other on the side of the devil, thus creating a double divide: the other is absolutely other, by virtue of moral discrimination, and he is on the side of Evil, thus of separation—*dia-bolos*. He is therefore doubly *other* in relation to me. Yet this does not exist in the human world, where no one is either an angel or a demon. The feeling of absolute separation that is expressed in hate indicates an understandable temptation—the victim's dream of confronting his abuser—but it negates the postulate on which human dignity is founded. If every man has dignity, I can hate no one, not even my worst enemy, since although an enemy, he is still human, like me, and is therefore like me by virtue of his intrinsic finiteness. I can hate only the devil incarnate, if he exists, for he alone is an absolute stranger to me.

The persistence of the Manichaean way of thinking that produced totalitarianism often seems to be the current prerequisite of all thinking. For example, in his most recent work, the former Gulag prisoner Gustav Herling expresses his astonishment that Evil has persisted even after the demise of totalitarian regimes: "it persists; it wasn't extirpated at the roots."[8] One day or another, everyone encounters evil, but most are not infested with it. "Every man is predisposed to commit a variety of acts, and one can't exclude the possibility that, on exceptional occasions, Evil will occur. Fortunately, you and I . . ."[9] Thus, there are those who remain innocent, even if tempted: you and I, of course, we who speak of it, we are innocent, but there are others . . . Despite the terrible experiences in Herling's life and his ability to distance himself from them in talking about them, he remains a disciple of Rousseau, perhaps without being aware of it: "The concept of original sin keeps us from confronting the problem of Evil."[10] He has rejected both forms of twentieth-century totalitarianism, yet his thought remains structured by their principal founding postulate.

Manichaeanism is revealed in the way in which our societies view and address wrongdoing. Indulgence for crimes committed on home soil, whether those of delinquency or corruption, is markedly on the rise, while at the same time anger is rising against international political crimes. This trend stems from two superimposed phenomena: political crime has acquired a metaphysical connotation, while ordinary crime tends to be blamed on the group. In both cases, as we shall see, personal responsibility is eliminated.

Hannah Arendt ultimately abandoned the idea of the radicality of evil, in the sense that Satan might inhabit human history: "I have changed my mind and I no longer speak of *radical evil* . . . at present, my opinion is that evil is never *radical*, it is simply extreme."[11] In other words, she came to reject the qualitative leap that would allow some people to be identified as demons, thereby separating them from the rest of humanity and making them responsible for earthly evil—hence her concept of the "banality of evil," which was to make her an outcast in intellectual circles after her essay on Eichmann was published. The virulence of this ostracism is noted in the correspondence between Arendt and Karl Jaspers, who describes one of her accusers as "a fanatic who lives behind veils of self-deception."[12] Her accusers "say of Hannah that she despises humanity"[13] and even suspect her of "excusing the Nazi crimes"[14] because she refused to acquit humanity by demonizing the murderers. In short, she preferred to hate the crime rather than the criminal, and therefore believed that the guilty can never be utterly equated with the evil they commit.

To reassure itself, late modernity in the same way radically isolates certain demons, which allows us to avoid having to face up to what is shameful in our history. We refuse to come to terms with this aspect of ourselves, to see these tragic events as part of our history, events that stand as evidence of our dark side. This is undoubtedly why those who have risked their lives in combat are admired only when that combat was against the Nazis and fascists—metaphysical criminals. Better red than dead, but better dead than brown. Those who fought the Nazis and fascists were angels struggling against demons. The enemy, on the other hand, those against whom one decides to take up arms, is described as the bearer of metaphysical evil, labeled Satanic, and portrayed with horns and pitchfork, like Milosevic.

The notion of metaphysical crime, oddly enough, reintroduces a spiritual category in a world unencumbered by God and devoted to the secular. It is as though the demonization of certain governments is the outlet whereby spirituality, albeit in negated form, lives on despite having fallen out of favor. It is as though Western societies, which cannot do without transcendence, have placed it entirely within the sphere of radicality in the form of the absolute evil of extermination. Transcendence, which millenarian doctrines had placed in a radiant future, is now present in the notion of a hell on earth.

In reality, we all belong to the same species. We are all capable of evil, which far from excusing criminals reestablishes them as responsible subjects. Their evil does not come from a nature distinct from our own, but from a moral laxity that leads them down the path of separation and hate. On the contrary, it is the demonization of criminals that excuses them, since it relieves them of responsibility by denying that they had freedom to act.

An analogous Manichaeanism can be seen in the way our societies treat ordinary crimes and transgressions. Since the nineteenth century, the philosophies of suspicion have undermined the responsibility of the subject, who supposedly acts either under the impulse of his subconscious (Freud) or under the weight of economic and social needs (Marx). Hence the rebirth of collective responsibility as a function of the group to which the individual belongs.

In totalitarian ideologies, the individual is guilty because he belongs to a particular group, not because of what he has done. Late modernity has not completely abandoned this way of seeing things: in any conflict between employer and employee, woman and man, delinquent and society, colonial and colonized, personal responsibility tends to be eclipsed by collective responsibility, which immediately decides who is the likely victim and who the likely culprit according to whether they belong to the previously designated victim group or guilty group.[15]

It is because evil is in each one of us, bound up in the expression of liberty, that we can become subjects capable of achieving an intimate, personal understanding of the difference between good and evil. As a self-aware and free subject, I am the source of my act. I am thus capable of a good and an evil for which society cannot be held responsible. Because man is neither innocent nor entirely dependent on his social conditions, he can lay claim to the status of subject.

We will be able to reconstruct a common world once we have admitted that evil does not have its source in a defined group, no matter what its definition might be: ethnic, social, religious, cultural, or ideological. Rather, evil emanates from humanity and is woven inextricably into the human fabric. But this certainty, the only one capable of keeping us from falling into the dangerous discriminations that foretell catastrophe, is not without heavy implications. It means that every human being is, so to speak, by nature or by inheritance capable of doing evil, but that no one is its creator. This claim is based on two premises: that man at birth finds himself conditioned by evil as well as good, and that he cannot claim total sovereignty over himself; he may approach perfection at the cost of immense effort but can never attain it. The creator of evil is not among us, for evil does not have a beginning—it simply is, and therefore neither does it have an end.

In order to reconstitute a world, if only through a rejection of the antiworlds bequeathed by the twentieth century, it is therefore necessary to stop personifying evil. A world in which we allow ourselves to identify Satan is no longer a world, for the angel of good and the angel of evil can never be part of a single entity. We must acknowledge the ubiquity of evil, because the rejection of the idea of original evil gives rise to Manichaeanism, scapegoating, and, ultimately, the splintering of humanity into separate species.

Nevertheless, the mental step of recognizing the ubiquity of evil seems to be extraordinarily difficult in our times. It requires a new vision of man, much different from that which has prevailed in the past two centuries. The dissidents of central and eastern Europe have been reflecting on this question for several decades and have condemned scapegoating as a philosophical deception.

The revolutions of 1989 in eastern and central Europe did not have as their sole purpose the toppling of communist governments. This goal represented only the tip of the iceberg. Their purpose was, rather, to lay to rest once and for all the foundational ideas of totalitarianism. And so what they went after was not a government or a seat of power, but the twin goals of re-creating human nature and personifying evil—ideas that are mutually sustaining. These revolutions were not "political" in the sense that their objectives were governmental, programmatic, or social: they engaged in "politics" as a consequence of deeper principles. Their real demand was above all to rise up from Manichaeanism, which for two centuries had singled out those who were guilty of human evil and acquitted all the rest.

The Czech dissidents of Charter 77, led by Jan Patocka, justified their fight against the regime less as a call for rights that had been trampled under foot than as a demand for personal responsibility. Where does the pervasive injustice in communist society come from? It could never originate in the "system" alone, for even if the "system" is perverse, this does not necessarily mean that its victims are innocent. The line between good and evil does not run between mistreated subjects and the partisans who mistreat them; it runs through each one of them. The primary concern of the dissidents was therefore not to overthrow the power structure and replace the tyrants with their victims. It was rather to figure out what could be done to prevent today's victims from becoming tomorrow's tyrants, should they come to power. Their concern was not to take revenge on History, but to put an end to the Manichaean logic that the communist era had propounded.

This was the first time such an intellectual step had been taken since the birth of Western totalitarianism. Communism fought against Nazism in order to replace one scapegoat with another. The postwar period saw the development of the same mentality. The United States identified communism as the personification of Satan—"The Evil Empire." This is what allows Francis Fukuyama to see the American way of life as a personification of historic Good— a way of life that is therefore unsurpassable. Today, many intellectuals in Western Europe are not antitotalitarian but rather only antifascist: They still employ Manichaeanism's intellectual framework and are thereby led to reject one form of totalitarianism while they whitewash another. In this respect, the dissidents of eastern and central Europe are the first to formulate an authentic anti-Manichaean, hence antitotalitarian, way of thinking.

Starting in 1989, one could see Polish dissidents newly in power working with members of the former government. In Czechoslovakia, one could hear Vaclav Havel utter the following sentence of capital importance: "Hundreds of thousands of communists do not constitute a species different from us."[16] If our post-totalitarian epoch indeed wishes to restore human dignity, it cannot go about creating new separations, but must rather proclaim the unity of the human species, despite the seriousness of previous wrongs. The discourse of this era allows us to see clearly that the problems of society will not be resolved by political revolutions. The approach taken by the dissidents of central and eastern Europe in 1989 serves to guide the twenty-first century into the philosophy of finiteness. That was made possible by the understanding that a human status which goes far beyond factions of opinion and confirmed crimes exists, namely, that all men are human to the same degree. Only with such an understanding can a human world take shape once again. The philosophy of rights is possible only if the dignity of each man remains independent of his crimes, just as it remains independent of his race, class, and his physical infirmities. To make human dignity contingent on good conduct belies an inquisitional mindset, instituting on earth hierarchies of humanity that only a celestial judge could properly describe.

It is this revolution, more philosophical than political, which allows us to explain the pardons granted to yesterday's butchers in these brutalized societies. Forgiveness is made possible only by recognizing the finiteness of the culprit, by holding deeply the conviction that, in spite of his crime, however heinous, he shares in the human condition. In the West, however, the category of the unpardonable—so familiar in our literature—reveals that we remain caught up in the snare of ideological Manichaeanism.

There is a profound difference at the present time between the West, which makes repentance obligatory, and central and eastern Europe, which grants forgiveness. Totalitarianism, together with religions that have lost their way and become totalitarian, has always demanded repentance as a condition for the outcast's reinstatement in the world. Forgiveness, on the other hand, is not the wrongdoer's reinstatement into the world but the affirmation that he has never ceased to be a human being; it is the recognition of his dignity beyond his transgression.

"If anything has remained of communism," writes Josef Tischner, "it is surely what it took to fight communism":[17] not the fight in the political sense, in the sense of the deposition of totalitarian power; but the philosophical battle, in the sense that communism gave the dissidents an opportunity to see through a mystification, of which communism represented only one expression among others. This mystification rested on the false vision of a world inhabited by angels and demons. This is why the "revolutions" of 1989 were not really revolutions, in that they were spared from terror and vengeance. They did not seek to upset the balance of power, but to break the fatal cycle of upheavals in order to introduce a common world, something that can be grounded only in the certainty of the ubiquity of good and evil.

The Manichaeanism that grew out of the modern philosophies of Rousseau and Fichte has given rise to secular personifications of perfection, just as it has given rise to secular personifications of Satan. If pure Evil can exist on earth, so can pure Good. Ideological systems thus take on the appearance of sacred and untouchable monuments, rendering an almost divine form of justice without themselves submitting to any law, fixed in a perfection that time cannot alter. We have come to understand the imposture of this sacralization of systems and institutions, as well as the behavior patterns that go along with it. Yet our realization of this deception has not borne fruit. Taking the small step of superficial rejection, late-modern thinking has rejected monstrous idols only to replace them with more attractive idols. The lessons of history, however, require that idolatry itself be rejected.

To leave Manichaeanism behind requires a new vision of the world, one whose various consequences are interrelated. The postulate of an original evil inherent in the human condition leads us to realize that good and evil are present everywhere, that we must not make the mistake of either demonizing or sacralizing any earthly phenomenon, and that our shared imperfection implies the necessity for respect. To live with finiteness calls for both attentiveness with respect to beings—even one's worst enemy— and distance with respect to things—even from one's most perfect achievement. Once the absurd futility of sacralization and demonization is recognized, our world will regain its immanence. Only in this way can our world aquire the means to really exist as a world.

CHAPTER 15
INTERIORITY AND ETERNITY

In the person-subject, a troubling and perhaps pathetic connection unites the self's unfathomable depth and its survival as a self beyond death. Few of us still believe in personal eternity, and yet no one can be unaware of how much the concept of personal eternity, in the history of our thought, has helped to establish the human being as an irreplaceable, unique being. The belief in the survival of an absolutely unique soul underpins the belief in the uniqueness of each being. And the inalienable dignity of the human being is founded on exceptionality: the human species is made up of billions and billions of exceptions. Every being has dignity because he is one of a kind.

The mystery of the human being is the reason for his interiority: the European culture of human rights focuses on man, as do all forms of humanism. It also insists on leaving him to himself, that is, on preserving his impenetrable interior life. It feeds the orphan, as any culture does, but it goes beyond this by forbidding that letters be opened and intimate thoughts exposed. In other words, it proclaims privacy as a categorical right and sets up laws in order to protect it.

The religious and ideological inquisitions infiltrated the depths of conscience, and in laying open the soul, they denied its reality. What then is to be made of today's society, in which the individual reveals his mysteries voluntarily? In the contemporary society of the spectacular, the individual is stranded between two shores: no one tells him what life means, yet he cannot find within himself the courage to defend and share, at his own risk, a meaning of his own choosing. He is left in a void. Yet life in society is necessary. The result is that his social bonds are superficial and without meaning. The individual lacking an inner conviction of truth has little more to say than what is conventional and socially acceptable. A constant flow of images protects him from silence and masks his boredom. The society of the spectacular is complicit in anesthetizing the subject, who, in any case, is not particularly keen on waking up and having to face the tragic dimension of life. But the society of the spectacular also helps the subject remain asleep out of fear that, if awakened, he might once again stumble into beliefs that could harden into dogmas. His superficial being guarantees contemporary man's harmless indifference.

Even glory, the epitome of recognition, needs no foundation in the society of the spectacular. It is enough to be *well known* to believe that one has gained *recognition*, as if outward appearance could somehow make up for the unreality of the subject whose feet never touch the ground. Our admired personalities are no longer heroes with a message or a mission. They are no longer persons of justice standing for an ethical principle. No, instead they are *stars*, models of human beings with no inner dimension, champions of the conspicuous and triumphantly visible. The star makes a show of his bodily fitness as well as the insignificant extravagance of his acts—like Alcibiades, who, in the age of democracy's decline, fascinated the Athenians with his beauty and casualness and his propensity for disparagement, which even led him to make decisions that were drastic for the city, all with the purpose of drawing attention to himself.

The person as subject evaporates amid the glory of appearance, especially in the exhibitionism and immodesty of a society in which display compensates for the absence of depth. The modest person is he who knows that he is endowed with more than meets the eye, and modesty is the mark of that privacy. The contemporary individual shamelessly exposes his feelings and adventures, boasting that he has nothing to hide. There is something pathetic about this self-exposure, which says, I am nothing more than this, this is all there is to see, since I swear that I have revealed the whole of my being. This is a dramatic and impossible poverty indeed: actually, every one of us is an iceberg with only the smallest tip showing. Prevailing thought applauds the desire for transparency, which it mistakes for grandeur, a refusal to hide behind a mask, a modern kind of courage with respect to oneself. And it mocks the modest person, who is now considered old-fashioned and prudish and is suspected of concealing shameful thoughts. The Incas ruled that windows and doors had to always be kept open so that government spies could at all times see and hear what was going on in anyone's home. Under Stalin, as in Huxley's *Brave New World*, the individual had constantly to expose every aspect of his life to surveillance. The total war waged today against hypocrisy is the unconscious heir to such demands because it is also the heir to an anthropological misunderstanding. Man is always more than he can show, and it is paradoxically his obscurity that reveals who he is. His secret defines him, and it is his nature to be indefinable. Personal depth is developed by maintaining the the tragic dimension of existence in which personhood takes shape; the encounter of the self with the self is perpetually carried out in the shadows. A conscience that lays itself bare disarms itself and ceases to be a conscience. The core of the person-subject resembles nocturnal demons that evaporate in broad daylight, disappearing before the eyes of anyone who looks at them.

Those who say they tell all and show all thereby admit their own emptiness, the narrowness of their consciences, and their banishment of the self-questioning and doubts that no one puts on display. These are individuals without self-doubt, without even confessed weaknesses, without guilt. Such immodesty reveals a person trying to rid himself of his own interiority. No KGB agent opens our private letters today, yet there is a longing for a transparent society without doors and windows, one in which mothers are pals, and lovers have no secrets from each other. The worshipped body, exhibited in its minutest wrinkle, reduced to its functions, becomes a lowly thing indeed, given over to its animality, ignorant of its own grandeur.

What becomes of meaningful silence amid the steady bombardment of words, so often as pompous as they are empty? What becomes of the body's vulnerability when it has been stripped and dissected down to the last pore? To those who claim to be able to articulate everything, what remains of the inexpressible mystery of human existence? The deception of sham appearance ultimately robs the person-subject of his uniqueness, leaving his very personhood in shambles.

Contemporary immodesty represents one of those apparently negligible aspects of social life in which the flight from the self can be seen. In the past, the subject abandoned himself to his ideology, his theories, and his systems; now he drowns himself in a wave of self-exposure and noise. Because not a single nook or cranny in which the subject's privacy is protected remains, his interiority finally disappears altogether—and with it, his identity. Today, opaqueness characterizes institutions as much as transparency does the individual. But the opposite is what is really needed: what is private ought to be left in the shadows, and what is public ought to be brought into the light.

Exhibitionism, an expression of both vanity and self-importance, becomes natural when living together in society is reduced to the mere appearance of what it should be. Beings cannot be bound together by appearances, which are created precisely in order to deceive the onlooker; appearances are pushed to the fore as a distraction from the fact that the inner depths of the human person are uncomfortable and unfamiliar. Or that those inner depths have been denied outright. In college, Gilles Deleuze taught us how to despise depth and to prize artifice. This is because depth is uncertain, a matter of faith, while passing phenomena are there for all to see. And yet the uncertain is what makes a world. Living together takes root in the word and in ethics. In early times, *logos* brought together beings who were scattered and separate, putting civilization within their reach; *logos* is the primary condition for the emergence of law. Ethics binds one man to another by respect, since an understanding of words is not enough for understanding another human being. Contemporary society makes a show of meeting these two require-ments of words and ethics, but in both cases it misses the mark because of a lack of substance. Contemporary society communicates without interruption, and without having much to say, since the quest for truth has been forbidden. Here, *logos* finds itself reduced to its outer form, to its mechanism; debate is clearly limited to deter-mining procedural issues, and dialogue becomes an end in itself.

We have trouble accepting that the subject might be alienated in any other way except as described by Marx or Sartre. That is why we discreetly cover up the alienation of the contemporary person. As the product of the relativism that grew out of the philosophies of suspicion, it results in a new deception. In the "postmodern" novel by Tomek Tryzna, *Mademoiselle Personne,*[1] the heroine, Marion, leads her life as an authentic person in a society completely given over to pretense. The cost is her inner stability. In society's eyes, she is "nobody" because she possesses only her soul—authenticity is noth-ing other than the soul—and the soul is imperceptible, shameful, insignificant in the world in which she moves. In plain terms, Marion says what she thinks and does what she says. Her existence *represents* her being, while her friends merely *simulate*, acting not to *express* or shape their own beings, but to *resemble* what it is suitable to be. Marion's words and deeds express what she is and the identity she creates for herself in the grand adventure of existence. The words and deeds of her friends, on the other hand, express what they claim to be but are not. In this deception, the subject comes undone. As a creature of the pleasure principle, he is unconsciously detached from reality. He is no longer alienated by overarching systems, by society or by "others," but by his own imposture. Because his action consists of pretending, he no longer knows who he is.

This expression of self-avoidance, characteristic of a society permeated by advertising, responds to the age-old and very human desire of the individual to be reconciled with himself. For what it always conceals is the anguish of existence experienced in its tragic dimension. The real aim of Marx the philosopher and reformer was to reconcile man with himself. Here, the utopias, which outlined how the human being and his desires might converge, agreed with him. This was possible, however, only at the cost of degradation, a staggering reduction. Contemporary Stoicism still hopes to eliminate the distance between the subject and his hopes, and to realize at last the perfect fit between man and his situation. But it is a perfect fit in which the subject breaks and dies, for he is a tightrope walker in a perpetual quest for balance, struggling against demons and exhausting himself in the effort to make sense of his life amid the anarchy of conflicting signs.

Is it any wonder that the new religious beliefs coincide with and legitimate the depersonalization and effacement of the subject? The person as subject does not exist in the Asian wisdom traditions; there, each being remains absorbed in the whole, from which he can distinguish himself only at the cost of being reproached for his arrogance. In the history of our own beliefs, on the other hand, appreciating the reality of the person as a conscious and responsible entity was made possible by the advent of God as a person. While the god of Aristotle was a principle, the personal God of the religions of the Book favored the elaboration of a unique concept of the human being. Here, man becomes a person, both as heir to the I-Thou relationship and as capable of autonomy by virtue of the distance he maintains within that relationship.[2] In the eighteenth century, with Deism, God once again became an impersonal principle, and nature was substituted for God.[3] Modern Western pantheism was thus inaugurated, and it finds expression today, after a long development, in the fascination we see for Spinoza and Asian thought, and more broadly in the widespread belief in reincarnation.

Little wonder that rejection of the biblical personal God has paved the way for the abolition of the personal subject. Since God was declared dead, modernity has given rise to depersonalization, which either stifles the subject—as in the totalitarian ideologies—or dilutes the subject—as in the present relativism. The fascist youth Thomas Mann spoke about has been replaced by the pantheist youth of our era. The religions of eternity heralded the survival, after death, of the person as person, with the self intact. In contrast, pantheism—as reflected in the belief in reincarnation or in a self-effacing oneness with the elements—abolishes the person by dissolving him in the whole. Pantheism thus guarantees an impersonal immortality: I survive death, but deprived of my self. And so it is that pantheism expresses the most recent manifestation of the flight from the self. The desire for release from the self and the abolition of the subject are integral parts of the one belief that still gives meaning to death: the absorption of the person into a sacralized nature. Pantheism abolishes death. In the cult films of Besson (*Le Grand Bleu, Léon*), immortal man becomes a dolphin or a plant.

The human dimension, however, lies precisely in the human being's mortality, which differentiates him from the animal world: an animal, as a member of a species with which it identifies completely, cannot "die" as a unique being, since it makes no claim to uniqueness.[4] The religions of transcendence saved the unique person by offering him eternal life after death as a unique person. Contemporary pantheism offers man immortality, but at the cost of sacrificing his uniqueness.

The spread of the religions of eternity was conducive to the advent of the idea of personal conscience. The belief in immortality through fusion with the elements bespeaks a regression of personal conscience and a skepticism concerning the uniqueness of each human being. Could a society like our own, so susceptible to pantheistic beliefs, still consider as its own the words from the Babylonian

Talmud? "For if a man strikes many coins from one mould, they all resemble one another, but the supreme King of Kings, the Holy One, blessed be he, fashioned every man in the stamp of the first man, and yet not one of them resembles his fellow. Therefore every single person is obliged to say: the world was created for my sake."[5] Will the certainty of inalienable human dignity be able to survive without the understanding of mankind on which it was based? That is the real question.

Is the current pantheism the logical fate of democracy, or is it rather a symptom of some democratic pathology? In a troubling prophecy, Tocqueville seemed to see it as both destiny and pathology when he wrote that pantheism, "although it destroys the individuality of man, or rather because it destroys that individuality, will have secret charms for men living in democracies. . . . Among the different systems by whose aid philosophy endeavors to explain the universe I believe pantheism to be one of those most fitted to seduce the human mind in democratic times. Against it all who abide in their attachment to the true greatness of man should combine and struggle."[6]

What is under debate here is the interpretation of human rights. I would not hesitate to describe the climate that gives rise to pantheism as a wrong turn of the Enlightenment. "Wrong" as understood with respect to the points of reference we so much want to preserve: the value of each human being's dignity, an idea that in our societies is now hanging by a thread. Human rights will not guarantee the dignity of each human being unless they are grounded in an understanding of man that ensures his uniqueness. There is an interdependency between religious choices and the choices of society. If one believes that democracy logically legitimizes an egalitarian individualism governed by common opinion, then pantheism supports and maintains this belief by expressing the egalitarian spirit in immortality—by crowning even in death an individual both similar to and undifferentiated from all others. If, on the other hand, one wants and hopes for democracy to be a society of unique persons endowed with free wills and minds, then the more appropriate religious partner would be a monotheism that preaches personal eternity, one in which each irreducible being survives in his irreducibility.

CHAPTER 16
CONCLUSION

During a trip to California, Czeslaw Milosz noticed this troubling graffiti on a wall in the university cafeteria at Berkeley: "Due to lack of interest, tomorrow has been cancelled."[1]

At the very end of a highly acclaimed book, the historian François Furet, so well known for his lucidity that some of his friends considered it a vice, wrote shortly before his death, "By its very existence democracy creates a need for a world ulterior to the bourgeoisie and capital, one in which a true human community can flourish."[2]

Tomorrow will happen anyway. Those who have not resigned themselves to the impossibility of achieving utopias will mark the memory of the passing century with their tragic immaturity. Their mark will soon fade: despair traces no path for others to follow.

The "true human community" is worth no more than a trinket reduced for quick sale at an old gag store. Democracy and capitalism are imperfect and, very fortunately, reformable, but they too will be replaced some day by institutions that will in their turn become obsolete. He who refuses to recognize his finiteness thereby removes himself from human history. The latest rebels may stop writing because they feel history has come to an end, but who will remember them when times passes them by?

The only "true" thing here below may well be the look of pure goodness that radiates from the face of a saint or just person. There is no *true* society. The only spark—and it is a furtive one—that evokes perfection on earth is always personal, never collective. There is no salvation by institutions. The future belongs to those who will work to promote the excellence of beings. Everything that nurtures the subject will also nurture society. The converse is no more than a farce drenched in blood.

The belief in collective salvation was the childhood illness of modernity. This belief has not yet surrendered. It puts forth its arguments right before the eyes of a blind public opinion, which has not recognized the old refrain sung to a new tune. This belief has the characteristics of a preposterous idea that suddenly made its appearance in Western history two centuries ago: the idea of justice without love.

A part of contemporary philosophy, having bitterly accepted the fall of communism, is occupied with trying to dismantle European culture by employing the same panoply of arguments eventually abandoned by the Soviets. The aims and method are the same, but the content is different. Society is still divided between the exploiters and the exploited. The exploiter is no longer the bourgeoisie, but rather the white European male, who holds oppressive values he believes are universal. The exploited are no longer the proletariat, but are rather divided into two distinct groups (although they are related insofar as they are both victims): women and the formerly colonized peoples. Women are described, following the example of the Marxist images of the proletariat, as purely negative figures, nonsubjects who are estranged from history and who have been deprived of a voice. They are capable of bringing about a revolution through the very nonexistence of their status, provided they become aware of that nonexistence.[3] The shift in the locus of the struggle and its extension from the social plane to the gender and international planes deepens the level at which the revolution is to occur. There is no longer any question of doing away with the state as an instrument of domination; the goal is rather to abolish the reality of the subject, because he might dominate others, and to abolish humanism itself, which, as anthropocentrism, manifests itself in male and European oppression.

Communism engendered arbitrariness and state cruelty by rejecting both law and morality due to their bourgeois origins. In the same way, the denunciation of humanism as male and European could result in a new dehumanization. While the stated aim is to defend the oppressed, the real aim is to destroy the oppressor, even if his victim is dragged down with him. This is more a matter of instituting hate than of trying to find a remedy for human distress: since in reality human dignity is respected to varying degrees, it is better to let an entire society be deprived of it, as long as its former oppressors are deprived of it, too.

The social dislocation that results when reality is increasingly seen in terms of the struggle between oppressors and oppressed expresses the will to do justice in a climate of hate, a will that was already at work in the totalitarianism of the twentieth century. Hatred of the "white male" paves the way for matriarchy and the rejection of humanism as a legitimate European philosophy.

It would be unreasonable to be overly concerned about this movement toward self-destruction, though. For by definition, it will destroy itself. The members of the Movement for Voluntary Extinction refuse to reproduce. Our commitment-phobic contemporary gives birth to orphans. He bequeaths them a sense of rights and entitlements and self-loathing, which does not amount to much of an inheritance. But what can someone who is burdened with resentment and rebellious desires invent? He will merely continue trying to deconstruct the world that has obstinately refused to consider itself a failed demiurge, in spite of his constant nagging for it to do so. Until he dies, he will merely continue to heap derision upon a humanity that is all too human, so that he can bury what he was unable to make immortal.

The future belongs to those who think that things mortal nevertheless deserve to be saved, who see culture as the art of living with mortality, and who revere the person-subject as someone who gives life to and thrives in this culture. These are the people who will care for imperfect humanity, since for them the mark of mortality is not repulsive, not the sign of some shameful disease, not a reason for scorn. They will usher in a mature form of modernity.

Gaining freedom from the old totalitarian regimes entailed institutional changes. Gaining freedom from the old ideological mentality requires inner conversion: it means calling an elemental, foundational hatred into question. Those who are singled out as the *oppressed*—formerly, the proletariat, now, women or the formerly colonized peoples—are not demanding the annihilation of culture just so that the oppressors will cease their oppression. What they are actually in greater need of is that we work toward a greater recognition of their status, which is what dignity really means.

To repeal the law of love-less justice is to rediscover our esteem for the human being, for that which we have neither created nor desired, for all to which we are the heirs, even if only reluctantly. No justice can be attained absent this paradoxical esteem for a being that is, yes, mediocre. The issue is one not of respecting human mediocrity but of respecting the unique being who bears that mediocrity. No humanism is possible for those who do not want to know who man is, who turn away from him in virtuous indignation and love him only as he might be transfigured. A humanist is not someone who reveres only his own theory of man. A true love of humanity consists in accepting the human person with all his frailties, and with the aim of sustaining his courage. It means acknowledging the dignity of the human being as he actually exists, not in his imaginary transformation.

We are so accustomed to cherishing only our ideas that we now seek, lantern in hand, those who are willing to love humanity in all its leaden heaviness, its terrible mediocrity, its ambiguous ways of life, its ill-adapted institutions, and its excesses—which always seem to end in near disaster. Will we be able to love humanity in its real misery, not in its dreamed-of perfection? This is perhaps the essential question, beside which everything else is merely idle chatter.

The process of abstraction that gave rise to the idea of justice without love is a process of suppressing human uniqueness, of imagining a man henceforth reduced and categorized, equated with the group to which he belongs. Paradoxically, conceiving human persons as atomized individuals sets the stage for this annihilation of uniqueness. To escape from the ideological mindset would entail a shift of focus: we would have to stop seeing the individual solely in light of the characteristics of his social, cultural, sexual, or behavioral group. We would have to see, first and foremost, the person and subject, and this according to the mysterious alchemy that makes him a unique being unfit for any reduction.

There is no ethic other than that of uniqueness, or particularity: the Good does not apply to concepts, but to beings of flesh and blood. Only an anthropology that sees humanity as consisting of unique beings can recognize the subject's autonomy, his ability to take risks, and his inherent responsibility. Destiny is not collective but personal. Responsibility is personal. Autonomy belongs to the self. Everything that is properly human escapes the collective domain. Only a unique being can be recognized as worthy of dignity beyond the various traits that define his group. Only he can be pardoned beyond his crimes. And only he can be loved as a concrete being. Abstract categorization produces Manichaeanism, imbecilic egalitarianism, and hate.

Hope for the future rests on the double certitude of man's frailty as well as his promise. These two certainties are interwoven opposites. To deny man's frailty leads to utopia. To deny his promise makes the certainty of his frailty lead to cynicism or inflexibility. A humanity that is marked by its failings can cling to hope only if it also carries within itself potentialities that are yet to be achieved.

The interplay of frailty and promise forbids us to dismiss all philosophies of man as illusory and compels us to reflect on humanity.

Because the human fabric remains imperfect, it cannot be reinvented by the will or indefinitely molded by desire. It commands respect through its weight and resistance to manipulation. We must try to understand this frailty before we can put a face on the promise. The presence of evil prevents the future from creating its own order: it must respect a certain givenness of being, which must always remain largely unknown.

The constitutive incompleteness of man forbids him to attempt to turn perfection into reality. But he can care for what exists, and it is probably this caring that defines what is uniquely and properly human. This style of being, as it were, expresses itself in the attention man pays to the world he has inherited in order to understand that world. The world we inherit and share is full of being, in the sense that forces are at work that we did not ourselves introduce. Having focused on reinventing the world, we must now turn our gaze toward the potentialities of being. Our fascination for planning must be replaced by attending to desirable possibilities. In order to care for, improve, and clear the brush away from what exists, we must keep in check our will to begin again *ex nihilo*, loving both existence and those beings who exist. That is, we must love them more than the products of our own minds.

The failures of the twentieth century reveal who we are. We are not demiurges. We are gardeners.

NOTES

1. INTRODUCTION

1. See Henri-Irénée Marrou, *Décadence romaine ou antiquité tardive* (Le Seuil, 1977).

2. THE INSULARITY OF THE HUMAN SPECIES

1. [Trans.] A play written by Jean-Claude Carrière, set in 1550 in a Spanish monastery, in which the debate regarding the humanity of Native Americans is reenacted.
2. Charles Darwin, *The Descent of Man* (1974 reprint of 1874 edition, Rand, McNally & Co.), 194.
3. Jacques Roger, "L'eugéneisme, 1850–1950," in *L'Ordre des caractères* (Vrin, 1989).
4. Hannah Arendt, "Le cas Eichmann et les Allemands," in *Ontologie et politique* (Tierce, 1989), 170.

5. André Langaney, "Les impossibles dans les origines du langage," *Pour la science* 211 (1995): 10.

6. Yvon Quiniou, "Darwin et la morale," *Le Magazine littéraire*, March 1999, 50.

7. On this subject, see Anne Fagot-Largeault and Geneviève Delaisi de Parseval, "Qu'est-ce qu'un embryon?" *Revue de métaphysique et de morale*, no. 3, 1987.

8. Sophocles, *Oedipe à Colone* (Les Belles Lettres, 1960), 393.

9. Peter Singer, *Practical Ethics* (Cambridge University Press, 1979), 75–76.

10. H. Tristram Engelhardt, *The Foundations of Bioethics* (Oxford University Press, 1986), 107.

11. Ibid., 218–19.

12. André Bichot, *L'Eugénisme* (Hatier, 1995), 76.

3. THE UNALTERABLE HUMAN FORM, OR THE LESSONS OF THE TWENTIETH CENTURY

1. Marcel Gauchet, *La Religion dans la démocratie* (Gallimard, 1998), 18.

2. Reinhart Koselleck, "Champ d'expérience et horizon d'attente," in *Le Futur passé* (Éditions de l'École des hautes études en sciences sociales, 1990), 313.

3. Nikolay Chernyshevsky, *Que faire? Récit sur les hommes nouveaux* [What Is to Be Done? Tales about New People]. This novel of ideas had great influence on Lenin.

4. Robert Redeker, "Des enfants de Mai aux enfants de Novembre," *Le Monde*, November 12, 1999.

5. Peter Sloterdijk, *Essai d'intoxication volontaire* (Calmann-Lévy, 1999), 14.

4. DERISION AND REVOLT

1. Gregory of Nyssa, *The Twelfth Homily on the Song of Solomon*, Song of Songs 5, 5–7.
2. Pierre Boutang, *La Politique* (Éd. Jean Froissart, 1948), 144ff.
3. François Furet, *Le Passé d'une illusion* (Robert Laffont, 1995), 572.
4. Francis Fukuyama, *Le Monde des débats*, July–August 1999.
5. [Trans.] *Pacs, mode d'emploi* (EOS Éditions, 1999), 27. The author is referring here to a recent French law that allows any two consenting adults to contract a mutual commitment and benefit from the fiscal advantages the alliance offers. Many believe that traditional marriage is undermined by the PACS.
6. Voluntary Human Extinction Movement: to become a member, "one must refrain from procreation," per the movement's Web site. See www.vhemt.org.
7. Sloterdijk, *Essai d'intoxication volontaire*, 26 and 15.
8. M.-O. Padis, "Les 20–30 ans: une cartographie politique," *Fondation Saint-Simon* (July 1999), 72.

5. THE TRACES OF A WOUNDED ANIMAL

1. Vaclav Belohradsky, "Sur le sujet dissident," *Le Messager européen*, no. 4 (1990): 23–46.
2. Milan Kundera, *Risibles Amours* (Gallimard, 1970). Published in English as "Edward and God" in *Laughable Loves* (Alfred A. Knopf, Inc., 1974).
3. Arthur Koestler, *Darkness at Noon*, trans. Daphne Hardy (Bantam Books, 1968), 137.
4. Ibid.
5. Belohradsky, "Sur le sujet dissident."
6. Predrag Matveievitch, "De la dissidence dans l'autre Europe," in *Fondation Charles Veillon* (Bussigny, 1993), 17.
7. As I reread these lines, I came upon a very similar analysis of the

same passage in the Declaration in Marie Balmany, *Abel* (Grasset, 1999).

8. Mircea Eliade, *Commentaires sur la légende de Maître Manole* (L'Herne, 1994), 245.

9. See my work *Les Idées politiques au XXème siècle* (Presses Universitaires de France, 1991), 87.

10. See Didier Éribon, *Réflexions sur la question gay* (Fayard, 1999).

11. Plato, *The Symposium,* 190c ff.

6. INSUFFICIENCY AND THE HUMAN WORLD

1. Aristotle, *Politics,* I, 2, 1252 a, 250.

2. Ibid.

3. Ibid., 1253 a, 25.

4. [Trans.] Professor Delsol is referring here to a popular music group in France called *Nique ta mère,* or Screw Your Mother.

5. Éribon, *Réflexions sur la question gay,* 184.

6. Cf. Jean-François Mattei, *La Barbarie intérieure, essai sur l'immonde moderne* (Presses Universitaires de France, 1999).

7. MUST THE SUBJECT BE SAVED?

1. Cai Hua, *A Society without Fathers or Husbands: The Na of China,* trans. Asti Hustvedt (Zone Books, 2001).

2. Ibid., 474

3. Ibid., 472–73

4. See Michel Rouche, "La famille matriarcale est-elle de retour?" in *La Famille, des sciences à l'éthique* (Institut des sciences de la famille, Bayard, 1995), 84.

5. See my *Les Idées politiques au XXème siècle,* 7ff.

6. Peter Sloterdijk, "Weimar et la Californie," *Critique,* nos. 464–65 (1986): 114–27.

7. Friedrich Nietzsche, *Beyond Good and Evil,* I, 17.

8. THE MODERN SUBJECT, OR INCOMPLETE CERTITUDES

1. François Furet, *Fascisme et communisme* (Plon, 1998), 62–63.
2. See Max Scheler, *L'Homme du ressentiment* (Gallimard, 1970), 150–52.
3. Alexis de Tocqueville, *De la démocratie en Amérique*, II, Chapter VII.
4. Thomas Mann, *Avertissement à l'Europe* (Gallimard, 1937), 30.
5. Eugene Ionesco, *Notes et contre-notes, La tragédie du langage* (Gallimard, 1966).
6. Ibid., 253.
7. See, in particular, the interpretation of Kafka's *Letter to Father* in S. Mosès, *L'Ange de l'histoire* (Le Seuil, 1992), 211ff.
8. "Communism is the resolved enigma of History and it knows itself to be such," Karl Marx, *Manuscrits de 44*, 3rd manuscript, IV.
9. Jean-Pierre Vernant, *Entre mythe et politique* (Le Seuil, 1996), 623–24.

9. THE FIGURE OF THE WITNESS

1. "Nothing . . . can possibly be conceived which would be called good without qualification except a *good will.*" Immanuel Kant, *Foundations of the Metaphysics of Morals,* trans. Lewis White Beck (Bobbs-Merrill Company, Inc., 1969), 1st section.
2. Stéphane Courtois and Nicolas Werth, *The Black Book of Communism* (Robert Laffont, 1997).
3. See Ilios Yannakakis, *Un pavé dans l'histoire: le débat français sur le "Livre noir du communisme"* (Robert Laffont, 1998).
4. For example, Luc Boltansky, *Le Nouvel Esprit du capitalisme* (Gallimard, 1999).
5. *De l'unique manière d'évangéliser le monde entier* (Le Cerf, 1990), 89.

6. Karl Jaspers, *The Question of German Guilt,* trans. E. B. Ashton (Fordham University Press, 2000), 33.
7. Claudia Moatti, *La Raison de Rome* (Le Seuil, 1997), 92.
8. Cf. Marc Heitz, "L'évaluation du bien-être: la perspective d'Amartya Sen," *Esprit* February 1999, 28–45. One could show how the concept of subsidiarity fits into this analysis.
9. Jan Patocka, *Essais hérétiques* (Verdier, 1981), 121: "Boredom is not a negligible quantity, a *simple mood,* or an intimate disposition, but rather the ontological status of a humanity that has completely subordinated its life to the day to day and to its impersonality."
10. S. Mosès, *L'Ange de l'histoire* (Le Seuil, 1992). Concerning Walter Benjamin, redemption could have intervened at any moment; "each second was the narrow gate through which the Messiah could enter."
11. Marie Balmary, *La Divine Origine: Dieu n'a pas créé l'homme* (Biblio Essais, 1993).
12. Ibid., p. 110.

10. COMMON VALUES AS LANGUAGE

1. Simone de Beauvoir has one of her characters say, "Defend a cause! We're not that backward. . . ."
2. [Trans.] The sociological reality of France is such that many of the problems Americans associate with the inner city—ghettos, gangs, and racial violence occur in the suburbs of France's largest cities.
3. "Ultimately, each postmodern tribe will have its own emblematic figure, just as each tribe, *sensu stricto,* possessed, and was possessed by, its totem. In all cases, identity, free will, decision-making or individual choice can of course be affirmed or demanded; but they are, in fact, subordinated to the identities, decisions and choices of the membership group." Michel Maffesoli, *L'Instant éternel* (Denoël, 2000), 42.

11. ECONOMICS AS RELIGION AND THE PARADOXES OF MATERIALISM

1. [Trans.] "Economic horror" is an an allusion to the title of Vivianne Forrester's French bestseller, which has been translated into English as *The Economic Horror* (Blackwell, 1999).
2. Radio Free Europe, Bucharest, October 21, 1998.
3. In the 1990s, "The real mechanism behind secessions is, however, not the defense of a threatened identity. It is the desire to no longer tolerate the shared life with others, since it seems more advantageous to live alone, to keep for oneself riches that are unduly shared with others." Pascal Boniface, *La Volonté d'impuissance* (Le Seuil, 1996), 115–16.
4. Psalm 49 (Revised Standard Version).
5. Moatti, *La Raison de Rome,* 42.
6. Ibid.

13. THE UNIVERSAL AS PROMISE

1. Condorçet, *Esquisse d'un tableau historique des progrès de l'esprit humain* (Flammarion, 1988), 269.
2. Jean Roy, *Le Souffle de l'espérance, La politique entre le rêve et la raison* (Bellarmin, 2000).
3. "In France, the International Federation of Human Rights, which is leading the pursuit, made a prize capture in early July by obtaining the arrest of a Mauritanian officer, based on the testimony of victims and by virtue of the international convention on torture." "La difficile recherche d'une 'justice sans frontières,'" *Le Monde,* September 27, 1999.
4. *Le Monde,* January 16, 2000.

14. THE UBIQUITY OF EVIL

1. Aristotle, *Politics,* V, 2, 1302b, 20.
2. Ibid., II, 5, 1263b, 20.
3. Johann Gottlieb Fichte, *Addresses to the German Nation,* trans. R. F. Jones and G. H. Turnbull (Greenwood Press, 1979), 179.
4. Ibid., 116–17.
5. Jean Elluin, *Quel enfer?* (Cerf, 1994), prefaced by Yves Congar and Gustave Martelet.
6. Aleksandr Solzhenitsyn, *The Gulag Archipelago,* trans. Thomas P. Whitney (Harper and Row, 1973), vol. 1, 27–28.
7. Pierre Assouline, *La Cliente* (Gallimard, 1998).
8. Gustav Herling, *Variations sur les ténèbres* (Le Seuil, 1999), 139.
9. Ibid., 156–57.
10. Ibid., 164.
11. Gershom Scholem, *Fidélité et utopie* (Calmann-Lévy, 1978), 228.
12. Karl Jaspers, Letter to Hannah Arendt, November 16, 1963, in *Correspondence of Karl Jaspers and Hannah Arendt (1926–1969),* trans. Robert and Rita Kimber (Harcourt Brace Jovanovich, 1992).
13. Ibid.
14. Arendt, "Le cas Eichmann et les Allemands," 171.
15. See. J.-J. Wunenburger, "Le procès de la responsabilité et les métamorphoses de la culpabilité," *Droits* 1987 (no. 5): 87–95.
16. Vaclav Havel, *L'Amour et la vérité. . .* (Éditions de l'Aube, 1990), 21.
17. Josef Tischner, *Esprits libres,* Spring 2000.

15. PERSONAL PRIVACY AND ETERNITY

1. See Michel Maslowski, "Le mal de ne pas être," in *Postmodernisme en Europe centrale,* ed. Maria Delaperrière (L'Harmattan, 1999), 171–85.
2. See Francis Jacques, *Différence et subjectivité* (Aubier, 1982), 86ff.
3. See Paul Hazard, *La Crise de la conscience européenne* (Boivin, 1935), 264ff.

4. Hannah Arendt, *La Crise de la culture* (Gallimard, 1972), 59.
5. Sanhedrin IV, 51.
6. Tocqueville, *Democracy in America,* vol. II, part I, chapter VII.

16. CONCLUSION

1. Rada Ivekovic, *Orients, critique de la raison postmoderne* (Noël Blandin, 1992).
2. François Furet, *Le Passé d'une illusion* (Robert Laffont, 1995), 572.
3. See Ivekovic, *Orients, critique de la raison postmoderne,* from Lyotard, Derrida, Serres, Sloterdijk, and Irigaray on.

INDEX

egalitarian individualism, 194
Eichmann, Karl Adolf, 94, 179
Elementary Particles (Houellebecq), 42
enemy, the, 181
Engels, Friedrich, 43, 62, 71
Enlightenment, 88, 95, 108, 162, 194
Entre mythe et politique (Vernant), 103
Erasmus, 91
eternity, 187, 193
ethical values, 114
ethics, 191; authentic subject and, 115–16
eugenics: basis of, 14; contemporary, 24–25; notions of personhood and, 18–19; scruples and, 54
European Union (EU), 143
euthanasia, 17, 25, 138
"everything is possible," 11–12, 23, 40–41
"Evil Empire," 184
evil: Hannah Arendt's sense of, 180; complexity of humanness and, 178–79; as conceived by Rousseau and Fichte, 174–75; as conceived under totalitarian regimes, 176–77; Manichaeanism and, 176, 178, 179–80, 186; necessity to stop personifying, 182–83; objectified, 88; as part of the human fabric,

182; perceived as a common heritage, 173–74, 186; as perceived in late modernity, 180–81; persistence after the fall of totalitarian regimes, 179–80; recognizing the ubiquity of, 183; scapegoating and, 175–76, 177; when personified in groups or individuals, 177–78
evolutionary theory, 13–14
exclusion, 93
exhibitionism, 190
Exodus, 165
experience, 32–33
experimentation, 32–33

F

faithfulness: to oneself, 81
family: Aristotle on, 58; changing notions of, 5; development of autonomy in children and, 77
fanaticism: as the blind acceptance of truths, 97; conflicts between identity groups and, 124–25; as the consequence of certitudes, 94; cultural relativism and, 123; dominant opinion and, 89; faith in transcendence and, 103; guarantee against, 104; human rights and, 106; origins of, 87–88; of particularity, 123; subject in the rise of, 106; universal cer-